The High Performance Blueprint

Strategies for Sustainable Success in Modern Organizations

Surbhi R. Bhosle

ISBN: 9798872887423

For permissions, inquiries, or bulk sales, please contact:
pokeme@surbhibhosle.com

Disclaimer

Purpose and Accuracy

The content presented in this book titled "The High Performance Blueprint – Strategies for Sustainable Success in Modern Organizations" is exclusively intended for informational purposes. The author has diligently endeavored to ensure the accuracy of the information contained in this book at the time of publication. However, the author explicitly disclaims any liability for any loss, damage, or disruption arising from errors or omissions, regardless of whether such errors or omissions result from negligence, accident, or any other cause. The author assumes no responsibility for errors, inaccuracies, omissions, or inconsistencies found within this work. The author and publisher disclaim any intention to offend or slight individuals, places, or organizations. Any such slights are unintended and regretted.

Case Studies and Examples

Case studies and examples, including but not limited to Microsoft, Satya Nadella, NASA, Spotify, NETFLIX, Toyota, Apple, and other companies and individuals, are employed as illustrative models to offer insights into strategies and practices for nurturing high-performance organizations. The author does not suggest that these are the exclusive methods or procedures essential for successful organizational management. Moreover, the examples provided are based on the author's interpretation of the practices employed by the companies and their leaders featured in this book. The information, analysis, and opinions expressed concerning these entities are rooted in publicly available information and should not be construed as official endorsements or representations of these organizations or individuals.

Content Reliability and Warranties

The author and publisher do not make any representations or warranties regarding the accuracy, completeness, or suitability of the content. The information in this book is provided "as is" and without any warranties of any kind, either expressed or implied.

Dynamic Nature of Business

The ever-evolving nature of businesses and organizational structures implies that the strategies and practices discussed in this book may change over time. Therefore, readers are strongly encouraged to conduct their own research and seek advice from appropriate professionals or experts before implementing any strategies or making business decisions based on the information provided. Neither the publisher nor the author will be held responsible for any claims, losses, risks, or any other economic damages, including but not limited to special, incidental, or consequential damages, whether directly or indirectly resulting from the use and application of the information within this book. The responsibility for any decisions made based on the content of this book rests solely with the reader.

Trademarks and Intellectual Property

Any trademarks mentioned in this book are the property of their respective owners. The use of these names and trademarks is strictly for illustrative purposes and does not imply endorsement by the respective parties.

The author and publisher acknowledge and respect the rights of intellectual property owners. Any use of copyrighted materials, trademarks, or other intellectual property within this book is intended for illustrative or informational purposes. Readers are encouraged to use their own discretion and judgment when interpreting and applying any content related to intellectual property within this book. The author and publisher disclaim any liability for any actions taken or not taken based on such information.

Legal Advice

This book is not intended to serve as a source of legal advice, and the information contained within should not be construed as an invitation to establish an attorney-client relationship. Readers are strongly advised not to rely on the information provided herein for legal matters and should always seek the guidance of competent legal counsel within their respective jurisdiction. The responsibility for legal decisions and actions rests solely with the reader.

Reader's Judgment

Readers are urged to exercise their own judgment and discretion when interpreting and applying the information presented in this book. The author and publisher disclaim any liability for any actions taken or not taken based on the information contained in this book. By reading this book, you acknowledge that you have read and understood this disclaimer and agree to its terms.

Contents

Preface

As a seasoned content writer specializing in Organizational Management and Human Resources, I have had the privilege of collaborating with numerous clients who grapple with challenges in sustainable performance and organizational excellence.

Throughout my career, I've delved into the critical elements of high-performance dynamics, spanning human resources, organizational culture, strategic management, and leadership, sharing the valuable insights gained through extensive articles.

'The High-Performance Blueprint' is the culmination of my experiences and extensive research. It aims to empower its readers with practical insights, valuable strategies, and effective tools for creating a performance-driven culture that relentlessly pursues excellence. The book is meticulously structured to comprehensively address this challenging and complex subject, covering every essential aspect for success.

While the strategies and practices outlined in this work offer inclusive and comprehensive coverage for becoming a High Performance Organization, it's important to recognize that they provide a broad overview rather than exhaustive detail. Successful implementation may require additional research and tailored efforts to adapt these strategies to suit your organization's unique requirements and preferences.

This book is designed to cater not only to senior leaders, managers, and HR professionals but also to individuals aspiring to contribute to a high-performance culture at any level. Its purpose is to encourage readers to adopt a fresh perspective on their role in this transformative journey.

I firmly believe that the creation of a high-performance organization goes beyond simply implementing operational best practices, policies, or processes. It involves creating a culture that embraces innovation, collaboration, and continuous improvement. This book serves as a roadmap toward achieving this goal, and I aspire for readers to find it both enlightening and motivating. I genuinely appreciate the time you invest in exploring these ideas. Wishing you the very best on your journey towards achieving all of your goals.

Surbhi R. Bhosle

Chapter 1 - Imperative of Building a High-Performance Organization

At the heart of every successful endeavor, there is an organization that thrives on excellence.

In today's ever-changing business landscape, organizations face constant challenges and uncertainties. The pursuit of excellence has never been more crucial, especially with the rise of globalism as businesses now operate internationally, tapping into emerging economies and engaging in cross-border trade. This interconnectedness has given rise to intense competition that goes beyond geographical boundaries.

The traditional reliance on a 'robust marketing campaign' proves insufficient amid these changed paradigms. To truly excel, businesses must continuously seek innovative ways to outperform rivals. The imperative extends beyond product/service delivery to encompass every facet of operation—cultivating a robust organizational culture, building an exceptional talent force, and maintaining highly efficient processes. The need for excellence in all aspects has become paramount in securing a competitive edge on the global stage.

To comprehend the shifts unfolding, understanding technology's pivotal role is essential. Digital transformation has thoroughly permeated every aspect of organizational operations. Technology has become the cornerstone of modern business practices, influencing everything from communication and data management to manufacturing, marketing, and customer interaction. Staying abreast of these advancements and comprehending their profound impact on the market has therefore become both integral and mandatory for successful business operations.

What's more, outdated technology has a noticeable impact on customer turnover. It is true that customers consider ending business relationships with companies that use obsolete technologies. Besides the concerns for security and privacy, consumers want to do business with companies that leverage technology to make their lives easier. On the other hand, businesses can achieve enhanced fiscal health by incorporating innovative software and technological equipment in their operations. This elevates the workflow and ultimately streamlines the overall efficiency, contributing to a more robust and sustainable operational framework.

Yet, its most profound impact can be felt within the realms of employee experience. In the quest to amplify productivity and efficiency, technology emerges as a critical factor in optimizing time and energy management, granting employees the luxury of pursuing creativity and precision. It enhances engagement by facilitating a collaborative environment, continuous learning and flexible work arrangements. Consequently, businesses are under constant pressure to keep up with the latest technological developments, influencing not only their product or service offerings but also their internal operations; failure to do so poses the risk of falling behind in this ever-evolving market.

But, the unceasing cycle of technological innovation demands more than just adopting new technologies; it necessitates the artful harnessing of their transformative potential. Consider Apple Inc., for instance. It not only embraced technological advances but also demonstrated a remarkable ability to transform entire industries with its ground-breaking products. When Apple introduced the iPhone, it did more than release a new gadget. It revolutionized the way people communicate, work, and entertain themselves. It seamlessly integrated a phone, a computer, and a music player into a single device, fundamentally altering the mobile technology scene.

Similarly, with the introduction of the App Store, Apple not just created a marketplace for applications but also fostered an entirely new economy. It empowered developers to create innovative software solutions and, in doing so, catalyzed the app ecosystem we see today. This illustrates that for Apple, it's not just about using technology; it's about setting a standard for innovative disruptions.

Now, let's transition to the next intricacy of the modern organizational dynamics. A trending complexity is the management of a diverse, multi-generational workforce, with each segment bringing forth distinctive priorities and motivations. For the first time in history, the workforce spans five distinct generations:

- The Silent Generation (1925-1945) is known for being thrifty, loyal, respectful, and determined. They prefer working within the system and highly value teamwork and relationships.

- Baby Boomers (1946-1964) are typically competitive with a strong work ethic. They place high value on workplace visibility, show loyalty to their employers, and many desire to continue working past retirement.

- Generation X (1965-1980) is often considered independent and skeptical. They prioritize work-life balance, display entrepreneurial qualities, flexibility, informality, and possess strong technical skills.

- Millennials (1981-2000) are confident, tech-savvy, and often seek creative work. They highly value meaningful motivation, work-life balance, teamwork, and regular feedback and are more concerned with intrinsic and moral values.

- Generation Z (2001-2020) is characterized as global, entrepreneurial, progressive, and less focused. They value diversity, personalization, individuality, and creativity and are highly skilled in using digital technology. They expect advanced technology in their daily lives and are known for their concern about climate change.

Please note that individuals from each generation may not universally embody the given specific traits. Our personalities and values are frequently shaped by external factors beyond our control, such as the circumstances we encounter during our formative years of life and careers.

As such, while it is important to refrain from making sweeping generalizations about individuals solely based on age, it is equally crucial to acknowledge that each generation's entry into the workforce is shaped by distinct factors. They include their era's social and political events, the state of the job market and technological progress, and the prevailing cultural norms. These factors significantly influence their sense of purpose, preferences, and motivations for success. Consequently, these unique experiences contribute to the commonalities that bind them.

For Millennials and Generation Z, who comprise a significant portion of the workforce, their professional pursuits go beyond financial compensation. They prioritize achieving a delicate equilibrium known as work-life balance and finding a profound sense of purpose in their careers. According to Deloitte's 2023 Gen Z and Millennial Survey [1.1], although nearly half of Generation Z and a significant majority of Millennials continue to view their jobs as integral to their identities, they prioritize work-life balance. This attribute is something they appreciate in their peers and is a foremost consideration when selecting an employer.

As a significant segment of the workforce adopts hybrid or remote work models and prioritizes flexibility, an escalating demand for such arrangements becomes apparent. This shift in work dynamics is reflected in the rising popularity of altered work hours and schedules, including options like flextime and compressed workweeks. Today, the workforce eagerly seeks employers who can enhance career advancement prospects for part-time employees, expand the availability of part-time roles, and offer flexible scheduling options for full-time employees.

The task of effectively managing the workforce becomes even more complex when you factor in the global talent pool. Here, regional, religious, and linguistic diversity play significant roles, adding both richness and challenges to the mix. As per a survey by the Pew Research Centre [1.2], a staggering 48 percent of Generation Z represents racial or ethnic minorities (as of in 2019 in U.S.). While this diversity can unlock innovation and creativity, it also introduces a set of hurdles, such as communication barriers, varying technology proficiency, cultural differences, and the potential for work-style conflicts. Thus, crafting productive and harmonious team dynamics in such an environment is undoubtedly a nuanced endeavor.

Moreover, the notable potential for differences and conflicts can pave the way for bias, discrimination, and harassment in the workplace. A survey conducted by All Voices [1.3] in 2021 (U.S.) revealed that 44% of respondents had experienced workplace harassment. This encompassed personal harassment, bullying, discriminatory bias, and online harassment. As such, building a culture of respect, empathy, and zero tolerance for discrimination is paramount. It is about finding the delicate balance between celebrating diversity and ensuring that differences do not hinder collaboration and progress.

In addition to these challenges, stress and anxiety loom large in the lives of the current workforce. According to Deloitte's survey [1.1], nearly half of Generation Z (46%) and four in 10 millennials (39%) grapple with frequent stress. These stress levels soar even higher among women, LGBT+, ethnic minorities, and individuals with disabilities. What fuels this stress is the amalgamation of financial and environmental concerns coupled with workplace pressures.

Curiously, the same study proves that despite their ardent desire for an improved work/life balance and reduced working hours, a significant number of Generation Z and Millennials find themselves shouldering additional part-time or full-time jobs to make ends meet. The pursuit of financial stability often drives them to stretch their limits. This heightened concern for the well-being of the workforce adds another layer of complexity for organizations to address.

Climate concerns are also at the forefront of career decisions for these generations. Over half the respondents [1.1] stated that they research a brand's environmental impact and policies before accepting a job, and notably, one in six has already changed jobs or sectors because of climate concerns. Thus, the ability to effect change on social issues can significantly affect recruitment and retention for these generations.

Let's now shift our focus to another critical facet of business: consumers. Today, consumer expectations have undergone a metamorphosis. Once relatively static, they've transformed as dynamically as the technological advancements they rely on. They don't settle for basic products and services, but crave experiences that seamlessly align with their fast-paced digital lifestyles. They expect organizations to meet their needs rather than anticipate them. Personalized solutions and minimal friction interactions across multiple touchpoints are the new norms.

According to Salesforce research [1.4], 66% of consumers expect companies to understand their unique needs and expectations, and 52% expect all offers to be always personalized. This sentiment shows that it's no longer enough to apply a "one-size-fits-all" approach—companies need to leverage data and behavioral science to determine what consumers wants and when they want it. Meeting these evolving expectations isn't just a competitive advantage; it's a driver of brand commitment in an era where loyalty is increasingly elusive.

After the extensive discussion of the complex business world, it becomes abundantly clear that achieving and sustaining high performance is a profoundly challenging endeavor. There isn't a single theory, model, or framework that can holistically address all the intricacies involved. However, in response to these challenges, the concept of a High-Performance Organization (HPO) has emerged as a promising model.

The notion of HPO serves as a framework that executives can employ to enhance organizational performance and sustainability. Moreover, it's flexibility and adaptability have contributed to its widespread acceptance. Unlike rigid models, this framework is not a set of instructions or a recipe to be followed blindly. Instead, it calls upon those tasked with its implementation to translate the framework into their specific organizational context, designing a tailored variant. It means the implementation of the HPO framework is highly subjective and depends on every organization's structure and performance drivers. This flexibility allows for the input of individual experience, expertise, and creativity, making it adaptable to various organizational contexts.

High-Performance Organizations (HPOs) represent a distinct category of businesses that consistently achieve excellence in both financial and non-financial results over an extended period. They surpass not only their competitors but also the industry benchmarks they set for themselves. HPOs aren't confined to the corporate world; they extend to government agencies, non-profit organizations, and any group with a mission to make a meaningful impact. These organizations have honed their strategies, cultures, and operational practices to excel in a myriad of dimensions.

André de Waal [1.5]*, a renowned expert in organizational performance, provides a formal definition* [1.6]*:* "A High Performance Organization is an organization that achieves financial and non-financial results that are exceedingly better than those of its peer group over a period of time of five years or more, by focusing in a disciplined way on that which really matters to the organization."

Intriguingly, research conducted by the HPO Centre, Netherlands [1.6] delved into the financial advantages of becoming an HPO. An organization can theoretically expect the following improvements versus its competitors when it becomes an HPO: Revenue Growth of about 4 to 16 percent higher; Profitability can be 14 to 44 percent better; Return on Equity (ROE) can have a 9 to 25 increase and Total Shareholder Returns can be 4 to 42 percent higher. Additionally, these high-performance organizations reported heightened customer satisfaction, enhanced loyalty, a notable reduction in customer complaints, more employee job satisfaction, and improved service and product quality. The data is unequivocal – the high-performance approach offers substantial practical benefits.

Let's paint a picture of these exceptional institutions. Think of an organization where every team member isn't just engaged but deeply committed to its mission, living and breathing its values and goals. Envision a workplace where innovation isn't a rare spark but a constant flow, where creativity isn't stifled but encouraged to flourish unrestricted by bureaucracy or tradition. Here, employees don't view their work as an obligation but a source of personal fulfillment.

Leaders in high-performance organizations are more than managers; they are inspirational figures who empower their teams to excel. They cultivate a culture of trust where accountability is encouraged, and the pursuit of continuous improvement is unceasing. But that's not all; customer satisfaction isn't just a metric here – it's a guiding principle, a north star that directs every decision and action. Such organizations do not resist change but instead actively seek opportunities to embrace and leverage it. They understand that change is integral to their growth and are quick to adapt and innovate in response to evolving circumstances.

So, in essence, what makes these organizations stand out are the distinct attributes that can be explicitly stated as below:

- **High-Performing Workforce**
- **Strong Customer Focus**
- **Commitment to Continuous Improvement**
- **Culture of Innovation**
- **Result-Oriented Approach**
- **Strong Leadership and Vision**
- **Adaptability and Agility**

Now, while these foundational characteristics mentioned are undeniably crucial in building high-performance organizations, it's evident that today's dynamic business environment demands an expanded set of attributes to propel organizations toward excellence. They must now be complemented by the following traits that address new challenges and opportunities.

Thriving on Speed: HPOs are not just accustomed to fast-paced environments; they thrive in them. Speed isn't a hurdle but a competitive advantage. They make swift decisions, adapt rapidly, and seize opportunities, giving them a distinct edge in dynamic industries.

Effective Knowledge Management: In a world inundated with information, HPOs skillfully manage knowledge. They optimize the use of information and expertise for decision-making, ensuring their decisions are informed, precise, and aligned with their strategic objectives.

Embracing Digital Transformation: HPOs lead the charge in the digital transformation of industries. They leverage technology to streamline operations and enhance customer experiences. Digital transformation isn't just a project; it's a fundamental strategy that ensures they remain agile and relevant in the digital age.

Championing Diversity, Equity, and Inclusion: HPOs understand that diversity isn't just a checkbox; it's a catalyst for innovation. They prioritize diversity and inclusivity, recognizing that diverse perspectives and backgrounds drive creativity and problem-solving.

Effective Distributed Team Management: As global connectivity reshapes the workforce, HPOs excel at managing teams across geographical boundaries. They've mastered the art of seamless collaboration, enabling them to tap into an international talent pool and enhance operational efficiency.

Commitment to Social Responsibility: Beyond profitability, HPOs embrace a profound commitment to social responsibility. They actively contribute to society and the environment through responsible business practices and initiatives, reflecting their holistic approach to success that extends beyond the bottom line.

While the concept of HPO offers a compelling vision for driving organizational excellence, let us also deal with the skepticism that might arise in the minds of those considering it. Concerns about the substantial time and resource investment required are valid, especially for smaller companies with limited budgets. However, the approach can surely be scaled and adapted based on an organization's size and capabilities. For instance, a startup or a company with budget constraints may need to adopt an incremental approach, such as:

- Focusing first on the 1-2 HPO pillars most critical to the organization's current challenges. For example, a start-up may emphasize building a culture of innovation and agility.

- Leveraging existing processes and structures before making major investments in transformation. Look for low-cost opportunities to increase performance through revised incentives or training.

- Scaling back plans to invest only in essential technologies and systems to support priorities. For example, Cloud-based tools can offer flexibility and cost-savings for software start-ups.

- Exploring industry partnerships, associations, and talent development programs to access resources and knowledge from external experts.

- Setting realistic phased timelines to spread implementation steps over several budget cycles.

While smaller in scale, these incremental changes can steadily align the organization with HPO principles. Also, the tenets of an HPO itself can help address the controversial aspects of its implementation. For example, although the cultural transformation may clash with existing norms in some organizations, change management techniques can ease the transition through transparency, open dialogue and focus on employee engagement. We will study change management in Chapter 4 - Change Management for Success in detail. And while realized financial gains may vary, research shows most HPOs do achieve significant measurable improvements. Developing a profound understanding of the pillars and practices of an HPO is important before starting the practical journey toward becoming one.

Embarking on the Path to High Performance

To truly comprehend the distinctive nature of High-Performance Organizations (HPOs) and their evolution, it is important to understand their journey. These organizations distinguish themselves from traditional or standard organizations by adopting a comprehensive and interconnected perspective when designing and managing their organizational structure. The process begins by defining the primary customers and stakeholders and genuinely understanding their expectations. In this systems approach, HPOs recognize that their organization is not just a collection of separate departments or individuals, but a complex system of interdependent components working together towards common goals.

They understand that various aspects of their organization, such as people, processes, culture, and technology, influence one another's performance and, therefore, overall success. Focusing solely on individual components without considering a holistic approach may limit the transformative potential. That is why they strive for a cohesive and synergistic approach. Here, their guiding principles, talented workforce, and efficient systems work together seamlessly, leading to exceptional results and achievements. Thus, in the process of crafting such an organization, it is of prime importance to recognize that meaningful and lasting improvements in business results cannot be achieved solely through isolated initiatives.

Aligned with this philosophy, this book introduces a systematic and comprehensive approach that encompasses six essential pillars, each indispensable for High-Performance Organizations:

1. People and Culture
2. Leadership
3. Change Management
4. Speed and Agility
5. Continuous Improvement
6. Knowledge Management

These pillars also serve as the organizational structure for the chapters in this book, offering strategies and practices essential for excellence in each area. While this work may not delve into every aspect of these approaches in exhaustive detail, it provides valuable guidance to set organizations in the right direction, significantly enhancing their chances of success.

Each chapter, referencing a specific pillar, offers substantial insights on its own. However, reading the chapters sequentially provides a deeper understanding of the systematic nature of HPOs and how each pillar aligns with the broader organizational framework. You may encounter some recurring suggestions, as they can contribute to strengthening multiple pillars.

To reinforce, remember that the journey of becoming an HPO begins by understanding the big picture. This book aims to provide a fresh perspective by incorporating many developments over the years and proposing a holistic framework resonating with the rapidly changing global marketplace, thus offering a contemporary understanding of HPOs.

Whether you're an experienced executive guiding a multinational corporation, a mid-level manager directing a department, an ambitious entrepreneur nurturing a startup, an HR executive shaping the workforce, or simply a curious observer of the business world, this book provides its readers with the knowledge and tools to navigate the intricate realm of organizational excellence. So, let's embark on this transformative path and unlock the potential for unprecedented success.

Chapter 2 - Cultivating High Performance

Unleashing the Power of People and Culture

Culture is the soil in which the seeds of high performance are sown, nurtured, and brought to fruition.

The success of an organization is intricately tied to its people, and the culture they actively shape plays a pivotal role in defining the values and behaviors steering that success. As a result, prioritizing investments in people and cultivating a robust organizational culture becomes essential to unlock the organization's full potential and achieve enduring success.

In HPOs, high-performing individuals serve as the cornerstone of their success, consistently delivering exceptional results through their skills, knowledge, and unwavering dedication. Their impact extends beyond their direct contributions, as they inspire and motivate their peers toward excellence. These high-performers encourage teamwork, creativity, and problem-solving, boosting the organization's overall performance. Additionally, having a resilient workforce helps organizations adapt successfully to uncertainties.

Turning our focus to organizational culture, it molds individual behavior and influences their workplace interactions. A strong, positive culture, deeply aligned with the organization's mission and values, instills a shared sense of purpose and identity. It sets up a framework that fosters collaboration and empowers individuals to proactively make well-informed decisions that align with the organization's objectives. Such a thriving culture amplifies employee satisfaction, ultimately leading to increased organizational productivity.

Furthermore, in today's job market, employees are increasingly drawn to meaningful work, consistent growth opportunities, and a positive workplace culture that extends beyond financial incentives. By strategically cultivating a culture that nurtures both professional and personal development, organizations become magnets for top talent. This approach sets in motion a cycle of excellence, where exceptional individuals accentuate the organization's performance, contributing to its long-term success.

This chapter explores strategies and provides practical insights for cultivating two most crucial assets: people and culture. Achieving exceptional performance is the ultimate goal, and regardless of whether you're directly involved in people management, this chapter is indispensable. Understanding the key principles outlined here has a ripple effect, amplifying impact across the board. Additionally, the chapter delves into the pivotal role of HR as a strategic partner in constructing High-Performance Organizations (HPOs). Let's start!

1 - Hiring, Retaining & Cultivating Top Talent

Securing and maintaining exceptional talent stands as a crucial pillar in the success of HPOs. A study conducted by McKinsey [2.1], involving over 600,000 researchers, entertainers, politicians, and athletes, revealed that high performers exhibit a productivity level 400 percent higher than their average counterparts. Similar results emerge in studies focusing on businesses, indicating that the productivity gap becomes more pronounced in roles with higher complexity. In highly intricate occupations, such as the information- and interaction-intensive work of managers and software developers, high performers demonstrate an astonishing 800 percent higher productivity. This research extensively highlights the significant productivity disparity between top performers and those with average performance.

While the advantages of top talent are undeniable, securing exceptional individuals remains a challenge. Organizations confront fierce competition in attracting and retaining these distinguished individuals, especially for roles that profoundly influence business outcomes. Furthermore, the evolving aspirations and expectations of the workforce, coupled with the escalating significance of inclusion and diversity, add layers of complexity to this endeavor. Hence, companies must forge a robust talent acquisition and retention strategy that effectively appeals to, nurtures, and retains top performers. Here, we explore several proven and effective approaches to consider:

1.1 - Attracting and Hiring Top Talent

Organizations can distinguish themselves as desirable employers by implementing effective strategies that encompass a holistic approach to hiring, ensuring a well-aligned and capable workforce. Below are some essential techniques that can help achieve this:

1.1.1 - Craft a Compelling Employer Brand

An employer brand functions as a mirror reflecting a company's identity, values, culture, vision, and mission, playing an indispensable role in captivating potential candidates. Its influence transcends beyond a mere logo or marketing campaign, encapsulating the overall reputation and perception of the organization as an employer. A robust and impactful employer brand effectively sets the company apart from its competitors, establishing it as the preferred choice for employment.

In the contemporary digital age, the significance of a positive employer brand is thus amplified, driven by candidates' unrestricted access to information. Prospective employees have the convenience to explore and gather insights about companies before embarking on any job opportunities. Authenticity guarantees that the representations and commitments made to candidates align accurately with the actual work environment. This congruence is crucial to prevent any discrepancies that could result in diminished morale, heightened turnover rates, and eventual reputational repercussions.

Employer branding covers various factors that contribute to a positive employee experience, such as workplace ambiance, company culture, guiding principles, and employee perks. It also involves opportunities for career growth and comprehensive initiatives for employee well-being, all of which collectively shape a compelling workplace identity. The convergence of these elements results in an appealing employer brand that attracts high-caliber candidates and nurtures profound employee dedication and engagement. With this groundwork established, let's explore the many benefits of building a strong employer brand and delve into practical strategies for developing and enhancing it.

Benefits:

Attracting Top-Tier Talent

A strong employer brand attracts individuals who share the organization's values. Candidates who strongly connect with the company's mission are more engaged with the job opportunity. This inspiration drives them to eagerly pursue and seize the opportunity to become part of the organization.

Building Trust Across

A strong employer brand engenders trust and credibility amongst the potential workforce and its other important stakeholders - consumers and investors. When a company is renowned for treating its employees well and providing a conducive work atmosphere, this positive reputation extends to the marketplace. As a result, trust is cultivated among all parties, making them more inclined to engage in business relationships with the company.

Decreasing Time, Efforts and Recruitment Costs

Earning a reputation as a distinguished "great place to work for" not only enhances an organization's standing but also draws in a broader array of qualified and genuinely enthusiastic applicants. Clearly expressing the organization's mission and values has a twofold impact: it resonates with not only proactive job seekers but also piques the interest of passive candidates (presently employed and not actively seeking new job opportunities but are receptive to the right one). This leads to a more efficient recruitment process, reducing the time and resources spent on building a candidate pool, sifting through applications, and conducting interviews that might not align with the organization's needs.

Increased Retention Rates Amongst New Hires

As mentioned, the authenticity and consistency that an employer brand displays, considerably reduce the misalignment in expectations of the new hires when they join the company. According to a study by LinkedIn [2.2], organizations with a strong employer brand experience 28% lower employee turnover rates than those with a weaker employer brand. This emphasizes the need to prioritize efforts toward building such a brand.

Strategies:

Build a Captivating Identity and Employee Value Proposition

To create a compelling and distinctive organizational identity, it is essential to acknowledge the unique qualities that set your company apart. This entails thoroughly evaluating factors such as company culture, mission, values, employee benefits, work-life balance, and other distinguishing attributes. Through an in-depth analysis of the strengths and weaknesses of your offerings, you can adeptly craft your employer brand.

Within this context, the Employee Value Proposition (EVP) takes center stage in defining your employer brand. It embodies the value your organization provides to employees in exchange for their skills and expertise. EVP goes beyond competitive compensation and includes other elements contributing to the overall work experience and job satisfaction.

Crucially, your EVP should seamlessly align with the needs and aspirations of both current employees and potential candidates. It's about creating a comprehensive package of tangible and intangible offerings that mirror your organization's identity and distinctive selling points.

Build a Strong Web Presence

It involves enhancing visibility and actively interacting with the audience on social media platforms, maintaining a modern and user-friendly website, regularly updating the job boards, and building a positive reputation on review and feedback forums such as Glassdoor [2,3]. Organizations should openly share their culture, values, and employee experiences to lay a sturdy groundwork for building enduring relationships. In this context, it's important to note that maintaining credibility hinges on the genuine portrayal of the employer brand alongside an accurate reflection of the company's culture.

Engagement with the target audience is paramount for establishing a robust online presence. It includes sharing industry-related updates, educational resources and actively participating in online discussions and industry events. For example, organizations can leverage engineering blogs to showcase their technical ability, thought leadership, and industry insights. By sharing valuable knowledge and expertise, organizations demonstrate their commitment to delivering value to their audience, positioning themselves as trusted sources of information.

Provide an Exceptional Candidate Experience

It is indispensable to create a welcoming experience for all potential employees. It ensures a positive journey and transforms candidates into influential word-of-mouth advocates. In the upcoming section, we will examine this topic in detail.

Cultivate a Nurturing Culture

To signify it, developing a positive and inclusive culture becomes the linchpin of the entire employer branding campaign, capable of easily shouldering its weight. We will also explore this subject later in this chapter.

Harness Feedback and Employee Advocacy

Conducting employee surveys yields valuable insights into your staff's perspectives, company culture, and areas needing improvement. This enables organizations to take proactive measures to create and maintain an engaging work environment. Moreover, by leveraging employee advocacy, organizations tap into their workforce's authentic and influential voices.

This can be achieved by harnessing employee testimonials, sharing company updates and achievements, and showcasing employee stories. By integrating the feedback from surveys with employee advocacy initiatives, organizations can craft a compelling narrative that connects with both current and prospective candidates.

◆◆◆

Case Study

Unleashing Success: Zappos' Exceptional Employer Brand

Zappos has not only achieved success in the e-commerce industry, but has also garnered a reputation for its strong and influential employer brand. Renowned for its exceptional customer service, employee empowerment, and unique company culture, Zappos stands out as an exemplary workplace. With its highly effective recruitment process and strategies, Zappos attracts top talent seeking a vibrant and engaging work environment. Let's take a glimpse at few of the efforts that the company has made to be an employer of choice:

The "Insiders" Program

In 2014, Zappos introduced a distinctive recruitment initiative called "Insiders" [2.4]. This program allows individuals to familiarize themselves with the company and establish a presence among Zappos employees. Instead of applying for specific job openings, candidates have the opportunity to engage in ongoing online discussions with recruiters. They can submit their resumes or LinkedIn profiles and engage with Zappos' team ambassadors-recruiters through various social media platforms. This initiative establishes a direct communication channel, allowing candidates to stay informed about the company's latest developments and unique culture.

Moreover, participants are encouraged to express their individuality by taking creative actions, such as uploading video cover letters and actively engaging with Zappos on social media. However, Zappos also respects the preferences of those who may prefer more private and limited interaction. As a result, this program enables Zappos to evaluate the alignment of candidates with the organization's values and workplace culture.

Social Media and Website

Zappos maintains a strong online presence across various social media channels, including Facebook, Twitter, LinkedIn, and Instagram. Through these platforms, it showcases its vibrant culture, values, and job opportunities. This active interaction with potential candidates promotes a spirit of community and engagement. For example, the 'Inside Zappos' [2.5] handle on Twitter is a window into its vibrant work environment, showcasing an insider's view. Additionally, it's LinkedIn page serves as a platform to showcase its brand and provides an authentic and transparent representation of the organization.

Zappos actively promotes the utilization of their branded hashtag, #ZapposCulture [2.6] on Instagram, where employees share images of their company outings and workplace moments. It has a YouTube channel called Zappos Stories [2.7], where they document the happenings of their workplace, sharing exclusive stories on employees, company culture, business insights, and how they deliver WOW through service to customers and communities. Moreover, its website's 'About Us' and 'How we Work' pages are engaging and informative enough to get a sense of how exciting working at Zappos can be.

Zappos Insights:

Zappos Insights, launched in 2009, is a distinctive initiative by Zappos that aims to share its unique company culture with the world. The program is rooted in the belief that a company's culture is the key differentiator between success and failure. It underscores the importance of identifying core values, hiring, and onboarding team members based on these values, and truly living by them. This approach allows the company to step back and let the team excel.

Zappos Insights offers a variety of services, including Company Tours, Virtual Tours, Q&A sessions, and Speaking Engagements, which provide an inside look into the company. Since its inception, it has successfully fostered lifelong friendships and connections. It has been pivotal in inspiring and motivating culture and values within various organizations.

In addition to these services, Zappos Insights also serves as a consulting arm where employees mentor other customer service companies on running contact centers and putting customers first. This department was created with the sole purpose of sharing the Zappos Culture with the world.

Zappos Culture Book and Internship Program

Zappos emphasizes its unique culture and values through the annual Zappos Culture Book, crafted by employees themselves. This publication features stories, quotes, and photos that vividly depict experiences at the workplace, showcasing the company's commitment to its employer brand. Furthermore, Zappos offers a comprehensive internship program that provides valuable opportunities for individuals to gain experience in diverse areas. Leveraging internships, Zappos attracts top talent and cultivates a pipeline for future full-time positions from within the company.

◆◆◆

1.1.2 - Create an Impressive Candidate Experience

A candidate's experience plays a pivotal role in shaping their perception of the organization, ultimately influencing the decision to accept a job offer. Previously, the primary objective for organizations was often to fill positions quickly. The emphasis was placed on their own needs and priorities rather than creating a positive experience for prospective employees. During periods of high unemployment or when there was a large pool of available applicants, employers had more leverage and were less attentive to this aspect.

However, the dynamics of the job market have evolved. Candidates now have more options and hold greater decision-making power. They can utilize online platforms, such as employer review websites and social media, to express their experiences and opinions about organizations. A negative candidate experience can quickly spread, causing harm to an organization's employer brand and making it difficult to hire and retain high-quality talent. To address this, consider implementing the following strategies:

Ensure Transparent and Prompt Communication

Keep candidates well-informed about the status of their application, give explicit instructions, and promptly address any inquiries they may have. Strive to make hiring decisions within a reasonable timeframe and communicate the anticipated timelines. This proactive approach helps manage their expectations and reduce uncertainty. A friendly and professional way of communication can foster a positive rapport and show your organization's unwavering commitment to transparency and attentiveness.

Convey Company Culture and Values Beforehand

Sharing information about your organization's culture and values in advance and encouraging its perusal allows potential candidates to assess whether their values and beliefs align with yours. One concrete method to do this is by creating an engaging and informative careers page on your website. This dedicated page provides a platform to communicate your unique culture and showcase the work environment, giving candidates valuable insights into what it would be like to work with your organization.

Also, implementing a referral program is a good initiative, as when current employees refer candidates, they tend to have a heightened trust in the organization. Referred candidates gain valuable insights into the company culture, work environment, and job expectations from the employees who recommend them. This insider perspective empowers candidates with enhanced decision-making capabilities, while also bolstering their confidence and comfort level throughout the application and interview phases.

Design a Positive Application and Interview Process

Pay special attention to user-friendliness and efficiency in the application process. A streamlined and engaging application experience sets the tone for a candidate's overall impression of the organization. Simplify the application by minimizing the number of steps and required fields and optimize the application platform for various devices.

Also, an interview process that is fair and transparent, and conducted in a supportive and professional manner is crucial. Ensure interviewers are prepared in advance and adhere to a standardized interview process. Additionally, incorporating interactive assessments or simulation-based tests adds another dimension to the interview process. This approach enables a practical and captivating platform for the candidates, enriching their experience.

Deliver Personalized Attention and Value

It is essential to enhance the interview experience by tailoring it to each applicant's needs and preferences. This involves incorporating personalized elements throughout the process. Consider the following efforts to create a more meaningful and engaging candidate journey:

- Adapting the interview format to accommodate any specific preferences expressed by the candidate
- Providing opportunities for candidates to ask questions and engage in meaningful conversations during the interview
- Sending personalized messages to convey genuine interest and appreciation
- Organizing meet-and-greet sessions with potential team members for first-hand interaction
- Designating dedicated points of contact to ensure seamless communication and support throughout the process

Another critical aspect is providing substantial feedback on candidates' performance, regardless of the outcome. It can include offering insights and advice related to their career development, sharing resources and opportunities for growth, and providing meaningful feedback on their performance. Demonstrating the value you bring to their professional journey establishes a strong connection and positions your organization as a trusted partner.

Craft Informative Job Descriptions

Providing a clear picture of the job's tasks, qualifications, and skills is crucial. It not only helps candidates understand the role better but also shows how this position fits into the team and contributes to the broader company goals. Moreover, presenting the organization's mission, values, and culture serves to illuminate distinctive and attractive facets that can capture the interest of prospective candidates. Highlighting the opportunities for career advancement and personal development within the organization further amplifies the appeal of the job description.

Also, offer information on the salary range, benefits, and additional perks. Although companies may choose to provide or withhold specific numbers based on their preference, offering candidates a general idea of the compensation package is advisable. It enables them to make informed decisions about their fit in the organization. Thoughtfully crafted and engaging job descriptions spark candidates' interest and serve as a valuable tool to assess how well their aspirations align with the opportunity presented.

Provide a Positive Onboarding Experience

Creating a positive onboarding experience is essential to help new hires reach their full potential immediately. By extending the positive candidate experience into the onboarding process, organizations can create a welcoming and supportive environment for new employees. Streamline the onboarding process by furnishing ample resources and training for job-related tasks. As part of this integration, acquaint new members with essential team members to foster a sense of belonging within the company's culture. Additionally, provide early opportunities for engagement and learning to ensure a smooth transition into their roles. While it may require significant effort, prioritizing this aspect is crucial as it yields substantial benefits.

Regularly Evaluate and Improve the Candidate Experience

Ask candidates to give feedback on their experience through surveys or direct conversations. When candidates withdraw from the recruitment process or decline job offers, conduct exit interviews. This feedback can provide valuable insights into their decision and also areas where improvements can be made. Similarly, after a candidate has been hired and onboarded, consider implementing post-hire surveys to gather feedback on their overall experience. It allows you to assess the effectiveness of your recruitment process, onboarding procedures, and the initial experiences of new employees.

1.1.3 - Have a Streamlined Hiring Process

Creating a streamlined hiring process is essential for maximizing process efficiency, minimizing time-to-hire, and increasing the chances of selecting the most suitable candidate. To attain this objective, organizations can implement the following strategies:

Identify Hiring Needs Diligently

Putting efforts toward identifying the talent gap will allow you to create a comprehensive hiring plan and minimize unnecessary delays. The following are its elements:

Conduct a Gap Analysis

This analysis involves evaluating the current workforce using data analytics to extract valuable insights. It also entails consulting with department managers and conducting employee surveys to further understand the requirements for new hires, upcoming projects, initiatives, and potential vacancies.

Moreover, collaboration with the training and development teams is vital to identify areas where current employees can benefit from upskilling or reskilling, thereby reducing the demand for new employees. By aligning the training initiatives with the identified skill gaps, organizations can maximize the potential of their current employees while minimizing the necessity for external recruitment.

Monitor Industry Trends on Skills and Technologies

Analyzing hiring needs within the organization is a necessary step. Moreover, organizations must proactively identify emerging skills, foresee future skill demands, and strategically channel efforts in these directions. This proactive approach is based on staying abreast of current industry trends, technological advancements, and consumer market dynamics. Additionally, benchmarking against competitors provides insights into skill gaps and areas where other organizations excel.

Imbibe Fairness and Consistency in the Hiring Process

Implementing a standardized hiring process significantly contributes to fostering objectivity and upholding a consistent approach to hiring. Take into consideration the following suggestions for implementation:

Establish a Structured Interview Process and Evaluation

This approach entails meticulous preparation, including defining the number and types of assessment rounds for each position. In addition, crafting a standardized set of questions for each assessment round is critical. These questions should be designed to assess essential competencies, qualifications, and experiences required for the role.

Equally important is the preparation of interviewers in advance and the strategic scheduling of their interviews. Comprehensive training in interviewing skills and bias prevention results in a high-quality and objective interview process.

Similarly, developing a scoring rubric or evaluation framework for each position significantly contributes to standardizing the assessment of candidate responses. This comprehensive framework should include specific criteria tailored to the essential competencies, qualifications, and experiences required for the role.

Interviewers then utilize these guidelines to assign scores or ratings based on candidates' demonstration of these attributes. This uniform approach ensures that all candidates are evaluated against the same benchmarks, facilitating more reliable comparisons and simplifying selection.

Conduct Panel Interviews

It involves the participation of interviewers from various departments, teams, or levels. This approach ensures a comprehensive assessment of candidates and facilitates collaborative decision-making. By including multiple perspectives, panel interviews objectively evaluate each candidate's qualifications and suitability for the role.

Develop Standardized Reference Check Procedures

This practice is essential to gather meaningful insights into a candidate's past performance and work habits. This process involves creating a standardized question set that effectively extracts consistent and relevant information from references. It is also crucial to guide those who are conducting reference checks, outlining the specific areas of interest and the desired information.

Use Technology to Improve Hiring Practices

Leveraging technology can significantly streamline the hiring process. Consider the following strategies:

Harness Automation

Organizations can explore using AI-powered tools for talent sourcing, candidate assessment, and interview scheduling. Implementing an Applicant Tracking System (ATS) can automate tasks such as resume screening and candidate communication, eliminating manual efforts and ensuring an optimized process. This approach saves time and reduces the risk of overlooking qualified candidates.

Capitalize the Power of Data Analytics

Data analytics offer a holistic understanding of recruitment strategies and outcomes, enabling informed decision-making and refinement of the entire hiring process. It includes evaluating critical factors such as job board effectiveness, identifying resource gaps, correlating interview questions with successful hires, assessing time-to-hire, calculating cost-per-hire, and analyzing applicant-to-hire ratios.

Embrace Mobile Recruiting

This involves optimizing job postings and career websites for mobile devices, allowing candidates to easily access and navigate these platforms on smartphones or tablets. Additionally, organizations can create mobile applications and utilize mobile-friendly platforms for seamless candidate engagement. Communication and updates can also be conducted through texts. These initiatives provide a convenient and efficient way for candidates to explore opportunities, submit applications, and interact with the recruitment process on their mobile devices.

Enable Virtual Interviews

Leveraging virtual interviews involves using video conferencing platforms or specialized interview software to conduct remote interviews. This approach accommodates candidates from diverse geographic locations, eliminating the need for in-person interviews and broadening the talent pool. Thus, virtual interviews offer the flexibility to consider candidates who may not have been able to participate otherwise.

Besides expanding candidate reach, virtual interviews save time and resources by reducing travel expenses and logistical challenges associated with traditional in-person interviews.

Despite the remote setting, this approach offers an opportunity for meaningful candidate interactions and assessments.

Incorporate Online Skills Assessments

This approach involves leveraging specialized platforms and tools to evaluate candidates' abilities and aptitudes. For example, software companies can use platforms such as HackerRank [2.8] or Codility [2.9], which offer online coding assessments for technical roles. These platforms present coding challenges to candidates, allowing for a remote evaluation of their programming skills and problem-solving abilities.

In addition to technical assessments, organizations can employ tools like Hogan Assessments or Myers-Briggs Type Indicator (MBTI) for personality and behavioral assessments. These online tools provide insights into candidates' personalities and behavioral traits, aiding in evaluating their fit for specific roles and team dynamics.

Continuously Evaluate and Improve the Hiring Process

A crucial approach to recruiting and retaining top-notch staff is consistently assessing and enhancing the hiring procedure. Here are several practical strategies to consider:

Actively Collect Feedback

Receiving regular feedback from hiring managers, candidates, and HR teams is vital for improving the efficiency of the hiring process. Gathering feedback on aspects such as communication, interview process, job offer experience, and quality of hires can shed light on areas for improvement. Thus, by valuing and incorporating the perspectives of key stakeholders, organizations can continuously refine their hiring practices and ensure they are aligned with organizational goals.

Leverage Hiring Metrics for Strategic Evaluation

Metrics, such as time-to-hire, cost-per-hire, and candidate satisfaction, offer quantitative and qualitative data to assess the effectiveness of the recruitment process. By scrutinizing these metrics, organizations can identify potential bottlenecks or areas of inefficiency that may affect the overall hiring timeline or cost and then optimize them.

Stay Up-to-Date on the Latest Hiring Trends

Organizations must stay informed about the latest advancements in recruitment to stay ahead in the hiring landscape. They can adopt the most efficient hiring methods by being up-to-date with emerging practices and tools. This proactive approach ensures they are well-positioned in the competitive job market and swiftly adapt to changing candidate expectations.

1.1.4 - Have a Holistic Assessment Process

Having an all-round assessment process is vital to selecting the ideal candidate who not only possesses the skills and experience but also aligns with the organization's culture and values. Organizations can employ the following strategies to attain this:

Assess for Culture and Value Fit

Besides assessing technical skills, evaluating candidates' compatibility with the organization's culture and values is crucial. It is, therefore, vital to incorporate interview questions and evaluations that directly address this aspect. During interviews, explore candidates' experiences and assess how well they align with the organization's values. Encourage them to share instances that reflect their ability to adapt and thrive within a similar work culture as yours.

Consider using behavioral assessments, such as personality or situational judgment tests, to gain further insights into candidates' values, work styles, and problem-solving approaches. Additionally, look for candidates who have successfully adapted to different cultures or work environments, showcasing their flexibility and openness to embracing the company's culture.

Assess Soft Skills

Assessing soft skills, such as communication, teamwork, problem-solving, and leadership abilities alongside technical qualifications, ensures the selection of well-rounded and equipped candidates to thrive in the organization. Incorporate assessments and interview questions specifically crafted to measure these skills. This approach enables you to accurately assess whether candidates possess the requisite interpersonal and communication capabilities required for the role.

Align Assessments with Business Goals and Objectives

Ensure that assessments for the open position are tailored to meet the organization's defined expectations and performance standards. This can involve establishing clear criteria and by involving key stakeholders in defining and refining evaluation parameters based on evolving organizational needs.

Similarly, before setting up interviews, reviewing applicants' profiles is advisable to weed out unqualified candidates at the start. It can save time for both the organization and the candidates.

Involve Multiple Stakeholders in the Assessment Process

Engage key stakeholders, including the hiring manager, HR representatives, and prospective team members, in the assessment process to achieve a holistic evaluation of their technical abilities, cultural alignment, and compatibility with the team. It is crucial to define specific roles and responsibilities for all stakeholders, regardless of whether they're directly involved in interviewing.

They can contribute to the design of questionnaires and assessment modules, ensuring a well-rounded evaluation. It helps significantly to use collaborative hiring platforms to improve communication and decision-making among team members working in different locations.

1.1.5 - Developing a Robust Recruitment Marketing Strategy and a Strong Candidate Pipeline

Organizations must develop a strategic approach to recruitment marketing and building a robust candidate pipeline system. Here are some effective strategies to consider:

Create a Comprehensive Online Recruitment Marketing Plan

Develop an all-encompassing recruitment marketing strategy, including tailored job postings, impactful social media campaigns, and targeted email marketing. Maximize the potential of popular social media platforms like LinkedIn, Twitter, and Facebook to establish an influential employer brand and actively engage with prospective candidates. Utilize these platforms to promote job opportunities, share relevant company news, and foster connections with a diverse pool of professionals. By leveraging multiple channels, you can effectively expand your reach and attract well-suited candidates to join your organization.

Implement Employee Referral Programs

Encourage your employees to refer qualified candidates by offering incentives and rewards for successful referrals. Leverage the power of your existing workforce as enthusiastic brand ambassadors who can bring in talented individuals aligned with the company's values. This cost-effective approach harnesses your employees' collective network and knowledge, enhancing the chances of finding exceptional candidates for the organization.

Actively Take Part in Job Fairs and Industry Events

Job fairs and industry events are valuable platforms to promote your company's unique offerings. They also help highlight career opportunities in the company, establish meaningful connections with prospective candidates, and network with experts and professionals in your industry.

Maintain a Talent Pool

Leverage talent sourcing tools like LinkedIn Recruiter [2.10] and other social media platforms to initiate and nurture relationships with prospects. Create a talent community by gathering contact information from interested potential candidates. Also, stay connected with promising candidates who were not selected or approached previously, providing them with updates on company developments, future job openings, and relevant information. It enables you to nurture relationships and engage with individuals who may be a good fit for future opportunities, ensuring a consistent pool of qualified talent already familiar with your organization.

Place Importance on Relationships with Universities and Colleges

Universities and educational institutions serve as significant talent pools. Establishing strategic partnerships with their career services offices, participating in career fairs, and hosting informative sessions can foster long-term relationships. Additionally, implementing internship and co-op programs offers students valuable hands-on experiences and insights into your organization's operations.

Such collaborative programs allow students to apply their knowledge in a real work environment while also allowing you to foster relationships with potential candidates early on. It also showcases your dedication to investing in the development of future professionals, which ultimately increases the chances of attracting top-tier talent.

1.1.6 - Offering Competitive Compensation and Benefits

Strategic implementation of compensation and benefits is paramount for building a high performing workforce. Companies aiming to secure and cultivate top-tier talent can leverage enticing financial incentives and valuable perks to create a positive and dynamic work environment. The tangible impact of financial motivation extends beyond mere appreciation, becoming a powerful expression of the value placed on employees' unwavering dedication and hard work. Furthermore, linking financial incentives to transformative outcomes equips executives with a potent tool for achieving successful organizational implementation (we will learn more about this in Chapter 4 - Change Management for Success)

In today's fiercely competitive job market, fair compensation emerges as a linchpin for attracting and retaining skilled professionals. It plays a pivotal role in enhancing job satisfaction and thus curbing turnover rates. Beyond addressing basic needs, compensation acts as a buffer against financial stress, empowering employees to concentrate on their roles. A thoughtful strategy, taking into consideration the cost of living, is crucial to ensure employees can sustain a quality lifestyle.

Compensation transcends its transactional nature, evolving into a form of recognition that shapes a positive work culture. Striking a balance between legal and ethical responsibilities in fair compensation is foundational. Yet, a holistic employee experience surpasses the confines of compensation alone, encompassing elements such as work-life balance, a positive organizational culture, avenues for professional development, and a profound sense of purpose within the company. This multifaceted approach collectively forges an environment where employees not only excel professionally but also thrive personally. Here are some practical approaches to contemplate:

Align with Business Strategy and Financial Objectives

A company's day-to-day operations are intricately linked to its financial goals, acting as the guiding force shaping its strategic decisions. Whether the emphasis is on cost minimization or talent development, it is imperative that the compensation strategy seamlessly aligns with these overarching objectives. For example, a goal centered around cost minimization might prioritize initiatives to reduce turnover costs, while a focus on talent development could prompt investments in comprehensive training programs. This alignment ensures that decision-makers are empowered to make informed choices that resonate with the company's strategic direction.

AA comprehensive evaluation of internal and external factors is essential when crafting an effective compensation strategy. Internally, it involves scrutinizing the company's financial health and its capacity to offer competitive salaries, ensuring alignment with financial goals. Externally, conducting market research to benchmark compensation levels for comparable positions becomes imperative. This dual-pronged approach ensures the formulation of a well-rounded strategy that not only aligns with financial goals but also maintains competitiveness in the dynamic job market.

Undeniably, a symbiotic relationship exists between a company's compensation strategy and its broader business strategy. Linking compensation to profits establishes a strong incentive for employees to actively contribute to revenue generation and the overall growth of the business. This alignment bolsters retention efforts and reinforces the integral connection between employee success and the company's overall success.

Furthermore, the effectiveness of your compensation strategy becomes a linchpin for competitiveness in the market. Striking a delicate balance between paying employees competitively and maintaining profitability emerges as a critical factor. Underpaying poses a risk to talent attraction and retention while overpaying may undermine profitability and overall competitiveness. A thoughtful compensation strategy takes into account market rates for comparable positions, offering a competitive salary that not only attracts and retains top talent but also ensures the organization's sustained profitability.

Develop a Comprehensive Benefits Package

To demonstrate your commitment to the well-being and satisfaction of your workforce, develop a comprehensive benefits package that goes beyond just a competitive base salary and aligns with the needs and preferences of your employees. Consider offering benefits such as health insurance, including medical, dental, and vision coverage. This approach ensures that your employees have access to quality healthcare. Retirement or pension plans are also essential components that enable employees to save for their future and be financially secure.

Paid time off, including vacation days, holidays, and personal leave, is another essential aspect of a well-rounded benefits package. Sufficient time off allows employees to recharge, spend time with loved ones, and maintain a healthy work-life balance. Other relevant benefits include flexible work arrangements, wellness programs, educational assistance, and employee assistance programs (EAPs). These offerings cater to the diverse needs of your workforce, keeping them happy.

Offer Performance-Based Incentives

You can drive employee motivation and inspire exceptional performance by providing performance-based incentives and tangible rewards, such as bonuses, commissions, and other profit-sharing programs. The concept of performance pay is pivotal for high-performing organizations, as it offers rewards that spur employees to enhance their job performance and elevate their productivity consistently. This approach acknowledges and rewards individuals for surpassing expectations, fostering a drive to excel and achieve specific objectives. Performance-based bonuses can be allocated at the individual, team, or company level, aligning with the overarching goals.

Furthermore, consider acknowledging and rewarding employee loyalty and long-term service through modern incentive programs such as Employee Stock Option Plans (ESOPs). By linking bonuses to well-defined goals and metrics, organizations can inspire employees to attain key results that contribute to business success. When implemented strategically, bonuses serve as a potent tool to synchronize individual performance with organizational goals, cultivating a culture of accomplishment and responsibility. Nevertheless, it's crucial to integrate bonuses into a comprehensive compensation strategy that includes competitive base pay and robust benefits to bolster employee well-being and job satisfaction.

Provide Opportunities for Professional Development

Investing in training initiatives and establishing transparent career advancement paths not only enhances the expertise of your workforce but also boosts employee retention rates. For instance, providing employees with the opportunity to participate in industry conferences and seminars facilitates the acquisition of new skills and enables them to network and cultivate valuable connections within their field. Such opportunities serve as powerful motivators for employees

Moreover, employers can implement tuition reimbursement programs for employees interested in pursuing additional degrees or certifications. This offers employees the chance to broaden their knowledge, advance their careers, and enhance their earning potential. Another essential aspect involves confirming that learning and development initiatives are attuned to the strategic objectives. We will learn more about it in Chapter 6 Driving High-Performance through Continuous Improvement.

Pay attention to Internal Equity

Organizations should develop compensation strategies to ensure internal equity, a vital aspect of fairness. Internal equity involves consistent treatment of employees in pay and benefits, considering factors such as experience, qualifications, and performance. This includes conducting job evaluations to determine position worth, factoring in job complexity and required skill levels.

Streamlining the internal equity of compensation significantly influences outcomes such as lower employee turnover and increased satisfaction. This is because a strong internal equity fosters a sense of fair compensation among employees, reducing the likelihood of them seeking alternative employment.

Convey Effectively and Be Transparent

It is essential to convey the compensation strategy to employees, offering thorough explanations of the reasons behind pay structures, the criteria for performance evaluation, and the methods used to determine rewards. Transparency in compensation practices plays a crucial role in eliminating perceptions of bias. This openness guarantees that employees have a clear understanding of the value of their compensation package and how it fits into the broader objectives of the organization.

Conduct Regular Salary Reviews and Surveys

Salary reviews involve assessing and modifying employee salaries within an organization. Typically conducted periodically, such as annually or biannually, these reviews consider individual employee performance, market conditions, and internal equity. They offer a chance to appraise the effectiveness of existing packages, identify any gaps or discrepancies, and make necessary adjustments to ensure fairness and alignment with organizational goals.

Similarly, salary surveys are comprehensive assessments of compensation data collected from multiple companies and industries. These surveys provide organizations with benchmark data on salary ranges, compensation practices, and benefits offered for specific job roles.

Comparing compensation against industry standards is essential for several reasons. It allows organizations to detect and rectify any imbalances in their pay structures that might discourage top talent from joining or staying with the company. Ensuring that competitive compensation packages within the industry and region is key to attracting high-caliber employees.

Also, organizations can proactively address any inconsistencies and legal or ethical risks tied to pay disparities by examining pay practices in the broader market. This approach helps reduce the risk of facing pay discrimination lawsuits and safeguards their reputation. Lastly, having a clear position relative to the pay market enables organizations to effectively showcase how their compensation practices are compared to competitors, thus building trust, credibility, and loyalty.

Conclusion

The strategies outlined above are essential to building a sound infrastructure for acquiring the best talent in the industry. Each approach plays a unique role in ensuring organizations can attract, hire, and retain top performers. Following is the review:

- Craft an impressive employer brand to showcase unique attributes and values.
- Create a captivating candidate experience throughout the hiring process.
- Have a streamlined hiring process for efficient candidate evaluation.
- Implement a holistic assessment process to identify the most suitable candidates.
- Develop a robust recruitment marketing strategy to engage with top talent.
- Build a strong candidate pipeline for a steady pool of qualified candidates.
- Offer competitive compensation and benefits based on market standards.

The following section will now delve into the strategies that can be executed to drive performance and achieve outstanding outcomes.

1.2 - Driving Results in High-Performance Organizations

A result-oriented culture is a pivotal and defining factor for organizational success. Such a culture represents an unwavering commitment to achieving tangible outcomes and fulfilling the core objectives of the organization. This means that a result-oriented culture is not just about achieving high levels of productivity and efficiency. Instead, it suggests that such a culture goes deeper, touching upon the fundamental purpose of the organization. So, it broadens the perspective on what success means for an organization, emphasizing the importance of making a positive and meaningful difference in addition to being productive.

Bringing up such a culture requires strategic approach that embodies a mindset and set of behaviors that are deeply ingrained within an organization's DNA. Why does this matter? Because a results-oriented culture not only improves operational efficiency but also enhances the organization's ability to adapt to dynamic and ever-changing business conditions.

At the same time, it drives innovation, and empowers employees to take ownership of their contributions. This instils a sense of purpose and unity, rallying the organization towards a common vision. Let's delve into some strategies and methodologies that can empower an organization to consistently drive remarkable results:

1.2.1 - Establish Cascading Goals with OKRs and KPIs

The concept of cascading goals involves breaking down overarching objectives into smaller, specific targets aligned throughout the organization. OKRs (Objectives and Key Results) and KPIs (Key Performance Indicators) are two essential tools in this process. By implementing this framework, organizations ensure everyone works towards the same goals and that their contributions are in sync with the overarching mission.

OKRs provide a structured approach for defining and monitoring objectives and their corresponding key results. Objectives here outline the overarching goals, while key results are specific and measurable outcomes, indicating progress. By implementing OKRs, organizations establish alignment and clarity across all levels of the organization. For example, an OKR can look like:

Objective: Improve Customer Satisfaction

Key Results:

1. Achieve a Net Promoter Score (NPS) of 70 or higher by the end of the quarter.
2. Reduce customer support ticket resolution time to an average of 4 hours or less.
3. Increase the number of 5-star customer reviews by 20% within the next month.

Simultaneously, KPIs are used to measure performance in critical business areas. These indicators offer a quantitative measure of success and provide insights into specific aspects of organizational operations. Engaging employees in the KPI selection process facilitates comprehension and motivation. This involvement empowers them to identify the metrics that matter most to the organization. For example consider the following KPI:

Key Performance Indicator (KPI): Monthly Sales Revenue

This KPI measures the monthly revenue generated by the sales department and provides a clear, quantitative measure of its performance. The goal may be to increase monthly sales revenue by a certain percentage or amount.

Thus, combining cascading goals, OKRs, and KPIs creates a powerful synergy for effective goal setting and performance evaluation.

1.2.2 - Provide Regular Feedback on Individual Performances

Managers can effectively address areas of improvement and offer actionable suggestions focusing on particular behaviors or actions that can be modified. Delivering feedback in a supportive and respectful manner is essential, as it encourages employees to be receptive and motivated to make positive changes.

In addition to manager feedback, organizations can incorporate 360-degree feedback as a part of their performance evaluation process. This approach gathers input from supervisors, peers, and subordinates, comprehensively understanding an employee's performance. By collecting feedback from multiple sources, employees can enhance self-awareness and receive a well-rounded perspective that facilitates targeted growth.

1.2.3 - Encourage Continuous Learning and Accountability

It is essential to empower your employees by providing the support, resources, and opportunities for their development in order to cultivate a learning-oriented culture. Additionally, establish clear expectations and align individual goals with organizational objectives. When employees know what is expected of them, they are more likely to take accountability of their work and strive for excellence.

Equally important is creating an environment that embraces experimentation and innovation, where employees feel psychologically safe to take risks and explore new ideas. In Chapter 6 – Driving High Performance Through Continuous Improvement, we will study all of this in-depth.

1.2.4 - Recognize and Reward Excellence

This approach underscores the vital link between individual contributions and the organization's overall success. It also creates a work climate where hard work and dedication are acknowledged and celebrated, motivating employees to excel. By aligning incentives with desired outcomes and linking bonuses, promotions, and rewards to the organization's goals, employees are encouraged to channel their efforts toward achieving those objectives.

1.2.5 - Encourage Self-Assessment amongst Employees

Motivate employees to participate in self-reflection and evaluate their performance. This involves employees reflecting on their accomplishments, identifying strengths and areas for improvement, and setting goals for their professional growth. By embracing this proactive approach to advancement, employees foster a growth mindset that prioritizes continuous learning and self-improvement. This mindset emerges from their recognition of the inherent value in driving their own progress through self-directed actions.

1.2.6 - Utilize Performance Management Software

Organizations can streamline operations, reduce administrative burdens, and optimize performance outcomes by utilizing performance management software. These softwares automate routine tasks, such as goal setting, progress tracking, and feedback collection. This automation saves time for managers and employees, allowing them to focus on more strategic activities, like coaching and development.

Moreover, performance management software enables organizations to collect and analyze data on employee performance. By centralizing performance data on a digital platform, organizations can gain insights, identify trends, and make informed decisions to drive continuous improvement. Incorporating this kind of technology also facilitates ongoing feedback and communication between managers and employees, fostering open and growth-oriented conversations.

1.2.7 - Assess Organizational Performance Comprehensively

The Balanced Scorecard framework is a strategic management tool that provides a comprehensive view of an organization's performance. It does this by considering multiple key performance indicators (KPIs) across different perspectives: financial, customer, internal processes, and learning and growth. This framework prompts organizations to balance their performance evaluation across these four perspectives, acknowledging that success in one area can affect the performance of others, ultimately leading to the achievement of strategic objectives.

While setting KPIs for different aspects of organizational performance is significant, using both qualitative and quantitative measuring approaches provides a holistic view of the organization's performance. Qualitative measures capture subjective experiences, such as employee feedback and customer satisfaction surveys, allowing organizations to understand the quality and impact of their efforts. In contrast, quantitative measures provide objective data, such as sales figures and productivity metrics, for analysis and comparison. By combining these measures, organizations can identify patterns, trends, and aspects that need refinement.

1.2.8 - Learn from Others in Your Competition

By benchmarking your organization's performance against industry peers, you can gain valuable insights and identify potential areas for betterment. For instance, study successful products of your competitors, their approach towards building them as well as their failures and challenges can inform your own product development strategy. Additionally, keeping an eye on emerging trends and best practices in your industry allows you to adapt and stay competitive. Attending industry conferences, participating in knowledge-sharing forums, and engaging in professional networks can also provide learning opportunities from experts and thought leaders.

Conclusion

Driving performance and exceptional results involves employing a wide range of strategies and practices. These encompass setting clear goals, offering constructive feedback, implementing a comprehensive evaluation system for individual and organizational performance, and ensuring appropriate recognition of employee efforts, among others.

1.3 - Culture and Values: Building High-Performance Workplace

Values embody the guiding principles and beliefs influencing an organization's decision-making and actions. On the other hand, culture represents a broader concept that encompasses shared beliefs, values, behaviors, and attitudes shaping an organization's identity. A positive workplace culture and a value-driven organization can enhance employee engagement, motivation, and productivity while bolstering the organization's reputation and overall success. Conversely, a negative workplace culture or the absence of clear values can lead to disengagement, increased turnover, and other adverse outcomes. It is imperative to focus on the following key elements for creating a positive workplace:

1.3.1 - Creating an Inclusive Workplace

Ensuring inclusivity is crucial for nurturing an uplifting workplace. It ensures that all employees, regardless of race, ethnicity, gender, sexual orientation, region, or religion, feel genuinely welcomed, respected, and valued. This, in turn, not only prevents harmful behaviors like harassment or discrimination but also significantly strengthens collaboration. To cultivate this kind of atmosphere, it's important to conscientiously adopt the following practices:

Establish Clear Policies regarding Harassment and Discrimination

Clear guidelines are essential for creating a safe and inclusive workplace. Craft these policies through collaborative efforts, seeking input from experts as well as involving your employees. Address crucial aspects like harassment, discrimination, workplace safety, and employee conduct to ensure comprehensive and well-informed policy development. It is critical to communicate these policies clearly to all employees, starting early enough during onboarding, and make them readily accessible through a centralized or physical platform.

Equally important is the consistent enforcement of these policies. By holding employees accountable for their behavior and ensuring that policies are applied consistently, organizations can maintain a fair and respectful work environment.

Provide Diversity and Inclusion Training

A diverse yet inclusive workplace requires ongoing efforts to raise awareness among employees regarding this sensitive topic. Providing diversity and inclusion training is an effective method for achieving this goal. Organizations should offer training programs covering important issues, such as unconscious bias, microaggressions, and cultural awareness at all levels. These training sessions help employees recognize and challenge their own biases, understand the impact of their words and actions, and appreciate the value of diverse perspectives and backgrounds. Ensure that training modules remain relevant and applicable by consistently updating them to reflect changes in the workplace and society.

Set Up Robust Reporting and Investigation Procedures

Facilitate employees with accessible channels to safely and confidentially report incidents of harassment or discrimination. Designated individuals or a dedicated reporting platform can achieve this. Ensure that employees are aware of these channels and are confident that their concerns will be taken seriously and handled promptly.

When a report is received, initiate a thorough investigation. Assign trained professional to handle such cases with sensitivity. Ensure that investigators follow an unbiased approach, gathering relevant information and evidence while maintaining confidentiality to the extent possible.

Based on the investigation findings, organizations should take appropriate disciplinary action if allegations are substantiated. This involves implementing corrective measures, providing training, or taking disciplinary measures against the responsible party. Ensuring that actions are fair, consistent, and aligned with organizational policies and legal requirements is crucial.

Offer Resources and Support to Affected Employees

The well-being and empowerment of employees who experience harassment or discrimination require a holistic approach. Here are key actions to consider:

Comprehensive Support

Offer a range of resources to support employees, such as access to counseling services, employee assistance programs, or external support organizations. These resources provide emotional support, and practical assistance to individuals who have experienced harassment or discrimination.

Ensure that employees are fully informed about the available support resources. This includes communicating the details of these services, how to access them and any related policies or procedures. Promote awareness through various channels, such as company-wide communications, intranet portals, or dedicated support platforms.

Provide a Conducive Environment to Seek Help

Establish a conducive atmosphere wherein employees feel secure and empowered to seek assistance without the apprehension of facing retaliation or judgment. Assuring employees that their concerns will be treated with the utmost privacy and sensitivity goes a long way in encouraging negative incidents to be reported and addressed.

Implement Initiatives to Promote Respect and Inclusivity

Leadership plays a pivotal role in setting a tone for a respectful and inclusive environment. Encourage open dialogues to address these critical issues and empower employees to bring their authentic selves to work. Implement initiatives, such as diversity and inclusion committees, employee resource groups, and town hall meetings, focused on promoting respect and equity.

Celebrate cultural holidays and events and showcase the achievements and contributions of employees from diverse backgrounds. Encourage initiatives led by employees that champion diversity and foster inclusivity. Remember, acknowledging the value of both - diversity and inclusivity - can build a strong sense of belongingness amongst your workforce.

◆◆◆

Case Study

Zappos' DEI (Diversity, Equity, and Inclusion) Initiatives: Fostering Belongingness, Empowerment, and Representation

Zappos is deeply committed to creating a workplace that values diversity, equity, and inclusion. A testament to this is Zappos' participation in the Valuable 500 initiative, a global movement advocating for disability inclusion in business leadership. Launched in 2019, the Valuable 500 encourages multinational companies with a workforce of at least 1,000 employees to publicly commit to advancing disability inclusion. In 2021, Zappos joined this initiative, aligning its entire operation, including employees, advertising, marketing, and products, with the principles of diversity, equity, and inclusion (DEI).

To further its DEI goals and enhance representation in career growth, culture, and community involvement, Zappos established Zappos One. This platform provides critical support to emerging teams and the diverse workforce within the organization, valuing and respecting individuals from a spectrum of backgrounds. Employee inclusion circles, including Zappos Asians and Pacific Islanders (ZAAPI), Black Awareness and Empowerment (BAAE), LGBT-Z, Women Empowered (WE), Women in Tech (WiT), and Zappos Organization of Latinx (ZOL), are central to Zappos' DEI initiatives.

These circles, led by dedicated members, create safe and inclusive spaces for discussions tailored to specific communities. By organizing events, workshops, and activities focused on personal and professional growth, education, and community outreach, Zappos strives to bolster representation and provide resources for marginalized communities in the workplace.

Acknowledging the significance of inclusivity among its emerging teams, Zappos prioritizes establishing of a welcoming environment for its entire workforce. The company understands that when team members are at ease expressing their true selves, collaboration becomes more effective, and their distinct viewpoints are valued. By promoting education and actively embracing diverse voices among their staff, it ensures that individuals from various backgrounds have their experiences, perspectives, and identities genuinely honored.

For ensuring equal opportunities and representation, it prioritizes continuous goal-setting, along with providing learning and leadership development opportunities at both individual and team levels. Thus, by actively promoting inclusion, empowering emerging teams, and providing safe spaces for underrepresented communities, Zappos aims to create a nurturing environment of belonging and empowerment, allowing all employees to flourish and contribute significantly to the company's enduring success.

◆◆◆

1.3.2 - Nurturing Holistic Employee Well-being

This approach involves creating an environment where employees are valued, supported, and encouraged to care for their physical, emotional, and mental health. Here are strategies for establishing such a culture:

Implement wellness programs

Introduce a range of well-being initiatives such as yoga or mindfulness sessions, nutrition workshops, fitness classes, employee assistance programs (EAPs), counseling services, mental health days, and other resources that can significantly contribute to employees' overall health and work-life balance. These initiatives prioritize employee well-being and create a supportive environment for both personal and professional growth.

Establish a dedicated wellness committee of employees from various departments, roles, and backgrounds. This committee will be responsible for developing and implementing wellness initiatives tailored to the needs of all employees. By involving representatives with diverse perspectives, the committee can provide valuable insights and ensure the relevance of the programs. It also promotes regular communication and feedback, constantly enhancing the effectiveness of these initiatives.

Promoting a Healthy Work-Life Balance

This involves providing employees with schedule flexibility and the choice to work remotely. It allows employees to manage personal responsibilities while fulfilling work commitments, thereby reducing stress and increasing productivity. Likewise, benefits such as generous time-off policies, paid leave for personal or family matters, regular breaks and vacations, and a strong emphasis on self-care collectively play a role in preserving a healthy work-life balance for employees.

Managers and leaders can themselves model healthy behavior by taking regular breaks during the day, leaving work on time, and setting clear boundaries around work-related communication outside of office hours. This will empower employees to prioritize their own well-being.

Foster Social Connections and Community Involvement

Creating opportunities for employees to connect and build relationships beyond work tasks is essential for a harmonious and productive workplace. By organizing social events, team-building activities, and mentoring or coaching programs, organizations can facilitate meaningful interactions among employees. These interactions cultivate strong social bonds in the workplace, contributing to improved mental health and a heightened sense of belonging among employees.

Encouraging employees to be involved in their communities through volunteering or charitable programs is a powerful way to inspire purpose and fulfillment outside of work. Companies can partner with local organizations or a cause to provide opportunities for employees to contribute to society. Recognize and celebrate such contributions on an organizational level. This way, employees develop a broader perspective, empathy, and a deeper connection to the world, enhancing their well-being.

Recognize the Value of Professional Growth

It entails offering comprehensive training programs, well-structured career development plans, and valuable coaching opportunities. By providing these avenues, organizations empower their employees to gain new skills and enhance their confidence to tackle complexities, resulting in greater fulfillment in their roles. Remember, when an organization invests significant efforts in providing growth and development opportunities, employees perceive it as a demonstration of the organization's dedication to their professional advancement.

Solicit Feedback on Wellness Quotient

Who better understands the intricate dynamics between the workplace and well-being than the employees themselves? Gathering employee feedback on their well-being at work allows organizations to tap into their collective insights, ensuring that well-being programs are relevant, effective, and in alignment with the workforce's needs.

Offer Healthy Food Options

Employees with access to nutritious choices are likelier to make positive dietary decisions, leading to increased energy levels, improved focus, and better overall health. Introducing fresh fruits, vegetables, whole grains, and other nutritious options empowers employees to make healthier daily food choices. Collaborating with local vendors or establishing partnerships with healthy meal providers can enhance accessibility and convenience, ensuring employees have easy access to nourishing meals and snacks.

Organizations can consider subsidizing the cost of healthy food options or providing incentives for choosing nutritious meals. These initiatives encourage healthier eating habits and yield long-term benefits for both individuals and organizations.

Create a Comfortable and Safe Workspace

By investing in well-maintained facilities and implementing safety measures, organizations can foster a workspace that supports employee health and safety. Ergonomic furniture, such as ergonomic chairs, adjustable desks, and well-designed workstations, promotes good posture, reduces muscle strain, and minimizes the risk of discomfort or injury. Additionally, maintaining a pleasant and well-lit environment with proper ventilation enhances the overall ambiance.

Similarly, organizations should proactively identify and address potential hazards, ensuring a safe working environment. Regular inspections, maintenance protocols, and prompt resolution of safety concerns are major activities. Providing comprehensive safety training and resources equips employees with the knowledge and skills to navigate potential risks and handle emergencies effectively.

Support Financial Well-being

Supporting employees' financial well-being is crucial for their overall happiness and peace of mind. Organizations can empower employees to make informed decisions and reduce financial stress by providing resources and benefits that address financial matters. Offering financial education resources such as workshops, seminars, or online courses covering budgeting, debt management, and retirement empowers individuals with the expertise and skills to make better financial decisions.

Organizations can offer access to financial planning services or counseling, providing personalized guidance and support to employees when facing complex financial situations and helping them set realistic goals. Similarly, retirement planning is a significant aspect of financial well-being, and organizations can contribute to this by offering retirement savings plans or pension schemes or by providing matching contributions and other retirement benefits, thus facilitating long-term financial security.

Furthermore, organizations can explore other financial wellness benefits that address specific needs and concerns. These may include access to discounted financial products or services, flexible spending accounts, or assistance programs to help employees navigate unexpected financial challenges.

1.3.3 - Building a Culture That Supports Organizational Values

In the pursuit of achieving the status of being a HPO, it's imperative for organizations to acknowledge the vital importance of cultivating a robust culture that fully embraces and reinforces their core values and mission. Such a positive culture not only fosters employee engagement but also enhances performance. Let's delve into the key steps and strategies required for ensuring this:

Define the Core Organizational Values

Establishing core organizational values is crucial as they act as guiding principles that shape employee behavior and decision-making. Devoting enough time and efforts to truly identify and articulate these values is therefore a necessary undertaking. Setting these core values requires a thoughtful and collaborative approach, taking into account the organization's distinctive identity, vision, and objectives. Here are some nuances and insights to consider:

Inclusivity and Diversity

Ensure that defining core values is inclusive and involves diverse perspectives. This can be done by involving employees at all levels representing different roles, departments, and backgrounds. Seize the opportunity to nurture a feeling of ownership and belonging among employees by actively seeking their input and feedback.

Authenticity and Alignment

Avoid simply selecting values based on external trends or what may sound appealing. Instead, focus on values that resonate with the organization's mission, vision, and long-term goals. This alignment sets purposeful aims for employees, motivating them and fostering greater engagement.

When values are directly linked to business objectives, employees clearly understand how their work contributes to the organization's success. This connection strengthens their commitment to the overall mission and purpose of the company. Authenticity in the values will help build trust and credibility both internally and externally.

Practicality and Clarity

The core values should be clear and understandable for all employees. They should provide practical guidance in decision-making and behavior. Avoid vague or overly broad values that may be open to interpretation. Instead, strive for values that can be applied consistently across different situations and contexts.

Consistency and Integration

Consistently communicate and reinforce the core values in all aspects of the organization. Integrate them into the recruitment and hiring process, performance evaluations, training, and daily interactions.

Review your Values

As your organization grows and encounters new complexities and challenges, assessing whether your existing values remain relevant and aligned with the evolving landscape is essential. Embrace a flexible mindset that allows for the timely adaptation and refining of the values, ensuring they continue to exert a meaningful impact.

Lead by Example

Leaders bear a significant responsibility for cultivating a culture aligned with organizational values. They must exemplify these values in their conduct, becoming living embodiments of the organization's principles. Exhibiting behaviors that are consistent with the values also showcases they hold themselves accountable for upholding these values. The leadership's demonstration sends a powerful message to employees, proving that the company's values are deeply ingrained in its culture and not just empty words on paper.

Use Values to Guide Decision-Making

To kickstart this process, organizations should begin by clearly articulating and communicating these values to all stakeholders. This approach ensures that there is a universal understanding of the organizational values.

Further, organizations should establish guidelines, standards, and criteria for decision-making that align with their values. This enables one to evaluate options based on their compatibility with the stated principles. Another vital step involves offering training and guidance to employees on incorporating values into their decision-making processes.

Recognize and reward individuals and teams that exemplify the values in their choices. This reinforces the importance of decision-making guided by values and inspires others to emulate these behaviors, fostering a deeper integration of the values within the organizational culture.

Integrating Corporate Social Responsibility

Establishing a culture that resonates with an organization's values in high-performance companies extends beyond internal operations. It must encompass the organization's broader influence on society and the environment. Corporate Social Responsibility (CSR) involves proactive initiatives that organizations undertake to address their actions' social and environmental consequences, transcending mere profitability. Here are a few key aspects of integrating CSR into your culture:

Align CSR Efforts with Organization's Values

CSR offers organizations a chance to align their stated values with their actual actions. It allows them to showcase their dedication to ethical behavior and sustainable practices, thus cultivating a culture that embodies these shared values.

Engage Employees in CSR Activities

This helps cultivate a sense of purpose and pride amongst the workforce. Employees become ambassadors for the organization's CSR efforts, driving positive change within and in the broader community. This engagement can boost employee morale, enhance retention rates, and attract like-minded talent.

Partner with Stakeholders for CSR Implementation

Implementing CSR initiatives in collaboration with customers, suppliers, local communities, and non-profit organizations builds strong relationships, fosters trust, and creates shared values. Such partnerships can lead to innovative solutions, enhanced brand reputation, and a positive societal impact.

Focus on Environmental Sustainability

Organizations today are increasingly adopting sustainable practices, such as reducing waste, conserving energy, and embracing renewable resources. These initiatives not only contribute to a healthier environment but can also result in cost savings and operational efficiencies.

Embrace Transparency and Accountability on CSR Progress

Organizations should be transparent about their CSR efforts and outcomes. They should regularly report on their progress, achievements, and challenges, demonstrating accountability to stakeholders and inspiring others to follow.

Conclusion

Cultivating a culture that upholds organizational values is far from a mere checkbox item; it is a strategic imperative for high-performance organizations. Building and maintaining such a culture requires commitment, consistency, and a collective effort from all organization members. Such a value-driven culture is the bedrock of success, fostering employee engagement and igniting performance.

◆◆◆

Case Study

Zappos' Core Values: Building a Culture of WOW, Creativity, and Long-Term Success

Zappos prioritizes culture above all else, focusing on its ten core values as the central guiding principles. The company fosters creativity, passion, and camaraderie among its employees, creating a distinct and lively work environment. It believes that a happy workforce naturally leads to exceptional customer service and long-term success.

Zappos considers its core values more than just words; they are considered a way of life. Initially, the company identified 37 beliefs as potential core values based on employee input. After careful consideration, these were narrowed to the final ten core values that now define Zappos' culture. These values are integrated into various aspects of employee experience, including the company's performance management systems, onboarding, and hiring processes.

These values serve as guiding principles for the company, dictating how Zappos interacts with its employees, customers, community, and business partners. Despite evolving processes and strategies, these core values have remained constant. They include:

- Delivering WOW through service
- Embracing and driving change
- Creating fun and embracing uniqueness
- Being adventurous, creative, and open-minded
- Pursuing growth and learning
- Building open and honest relationships through communication
- Fostering a positive team and family spirit
- Doing more with less
- Being passionate and determined
- Embracing humility

Zappos conducts a distinctive onboarding program to familiarize new employees with the company's culture and core values. This program begins with a four-week Customer Loyalty Team (CLT) training, during which employees learn about the company's history, culture, and core values. Regardless of their title, every employee is required to shadow the Customer Loyalty Team and answer phone calls, providing them with firsthand experience of Zappos' customer-centric approach.

Following the training, Zappos offers a unique option called "Pay to Quit." If new employees do not feel like they fit in with the company culture, they have the option to resign and receive a specific amount of compensation. By adopting this method, Zappos guarantees that the employees who choose to stay, genuinely embody and embrace the company's values.

Additionally, the onboarding program includes on-the-job training to develop new employees' skills and knowledge. To celebrate their completion of the onboarding process, Zappos hosts a graduation party. These elements of the program aim to create an immersive onboarding experience that not only benefits new employees but also contributes to the overall success of the company.

Zappos firmly believes that by establishing a thriving culture, other aspects, such as exceptional customer service, long-term brand building, and business success, will naturally follow. This belief has driven the company to create a culture that celebrates individuality, creativity, and humor. Zappos makes sure that its employees match its core values by hiring based on cultural fit along with technical skills. This intentional focus on culture has been instrumental in shaping Zappos' success.

The company's rigorous approach includes multiple rounds of interviews with diverse team members. These interviews not only evaluate candidates' technical proficiency but also assess their compatibility with culture. They conduct interviews based on a set of behaviorally based questions that delve into each candidate's congruence with the core values. By involving various team members in the assessment, Zappos ensures a comprehensive evaluation. Furthermore, there is facilitation of social interactions between candidates and current employees. This approach allows both parties to gauge compatibility and establish rapport.

In 2014, the company also implemented Holacracy, a self-managed organizational structure. Holacracy is a system of corporate governance that disperses authority and decision-making across the organization rather than concentrating it within a traditional management hierarchy. At Zappos, this approach empowers employees to pinpoint opportunities for improvement and suggest solutions. Self-management entails a clear understanding of one's specific responsibilities and the autonomy to fulfill them in the manner that aligns best with individual judgment. Since implementing Holacracy, Zappos has been continuously fine-tuning the system to align it with their culture, core values, and focus on people. This customization ensures that the system fits their unique requirements.

◆◆◆

2 - HR as a Strategic Partner

HR has emerged as a strategic partner, moving beyond administrative tasks and driving organizational success. This shift reflects the growing understanding that people are the most valuable asset of any organization, and HR professionals possess a unique set of skills and abilities that enable them to align this human capital with business objectives.

The evolution of Human Resources (HR) as a strategic partner has been a dynamic process influenced by various factors, such as changes in the business environment, advancements in technology, and shifts in organizational priorities. In the early stages of HR development, which predates the 20th century, the function was primarily administrative. HR's core responsibilities included managing payroll, maintaining personnel records, and ensuring compliance with labor laws. During this period, HR operated in a transactional and reactive mode, concentrating on immediate operational needs rather than strategic, long-term planning. The function's primary goal was the smooth execution of administrative tasks to support day-to-day operations.

As industrialization gained momentum in the early to mid-20th century, HR transitioned into personnel management. This era was characterized by an increased emphasis on employee welfare and strict adherence to evolving labor laws. The emergence of dedicated personnel departments aimed to systematize routine tasks such as hiring, firing, and managing employee relations. However, strategic impact remained limited, as the predominant focus was on regulatory compliance rather than aligning HR practices with broader business objectives.

The mid-20th century marked a pivotal shift with the advent of Human Resource Management (HRM). This phase brought about a more holistic approach to managing people within organizations. HRM expanded its scope to include recruitment, training, and performance management activities. A key development during this period was the growing recognition of aligning human capital with organizational goals. This shift reflected an initial move towards a more strategic mindset within the HR function.

In the latter part of the 20th century, HR underwent a profound transformation into a strategic partner. Influenced by management theories, particularly those related to strategic management, HR professionals started actively aligning their activities with the overarching business strategy. This shift represented a departure from a purely administrative role to one where HR played an instrumental part in achieving organizational success. Integration of HR practices with broader business goals became a defining characteristic of this period.

The late 20th century and beyond witnessed the consolidation of HR as a strategic business partner. HR professionals became indispensable in strategic decision-making processes, with a pronounced focus on talent management, leadership development, and workforce planning. This era saw a paradigm shift where HR practices were not merely aligned but directly contributed to the realization of business objectives.

In the 21st century, the evolution of HR continued with the widespread adoption of advanced technologies. Automation and data-driven decision-making became integral components of HR functions. This technological integration empowered HR to make more informed and strategic choices. The use of HR information systems, generative AI and analytics tools enabled a more agile and responsive HR function capable of adapting to the rapidly changing business landscape.

In the contemporary HR landscape, there is a notable shift towards enhancing the overall employee experience. A HR partner is now expected to play a pivotal role in creating a sustainable and healthy workplace environment, recognizing the intricate link between employee well-being and overall performance.

Looking into the future, the evolution of HR is expected to involve even greater agility and adaptability. While advanced technology remains a crucial component, there is also a growing recognition of the importance of a return to a more human-centric approach. Emerging businesses often exemplify this future trend, emphasizing agility over rigid processes and fostering a workplace culture that prioritizes individual growth and well-being.

Simultaneously, simplification is emerging as another significant HR trend. Running a complex organization with sophisticated HR processes is perceived as expensive and potentially hindering competitiveness. A complex and slow decision-making process, influenced by multiple layers of governance or management, can hinder an organization's competitiveness.

Organizations should now be emphasizing the need to become quick and lean. HR is therefore expected to focus on simplifying its complex processes, returning decision-making to employees. Although this shift may pose initial challenges, embracing this initiative is crucial, given its extensive and enduring positive impact on organizational performance.

HR's strategic partnership today encompasses a comprehensive spectrum of areas within an organization, ensuring a holistic approach to human capital management. These areas include but are not limited to:

Talent Management:

- Recruitment and Onboarding: Attracting and selecting top talent aligned with organizational needs.

- Workforce Planning: Anticipating and addressing future skill requirements through strategic planning.

- Succession Planning: Identifying and developing potential leaders to ensure a smooth transition in key roles.

Leadership Development:

- Leadership Programs: Designing initiatives to cultivate leadership skills and competencies.

- Mentorship and Coaching: Providing support systems for current and emerging leaders to enhance their capabilities.

-Leadership Succession: Ensuring a pipeline of skilled leaders ready to step into critical roles.

Employee Engagement:

- Cultural Alignment: Fostering a positive workplace culture that aligns with organizational values.

- Well-being Initiatives: Implementing programs that address employees' holistic needs and enhance overall well-being.

- Communication Strategies: Ensuring effective communication to foster engagement and alignment with organizational goals.

Performance Management:

- Goal Alignment: Aligning individual and team performance goals with organizational objectives.

- Feedback Mechanisms: Establishing regular feedback loops for continuous performance improvement.

- Recognition Programs: Implementing strategic employee recognition initiatives tied to organizational success.

Organizational Culture:

- Cultural Transformation: Leading efforts to shape and evolve the organizational culture.

- Diversity and Inclusion: Promoting a diverse and inclusive workplace that reflects the organization's values.

- Values Integration: Embedding core values into daily operations to guide employee behavior.

Change Management:

- Adaptive Workflows: Navigating change by embracing adaptive and flexible HR processes.

- Employee Advocacy: Creating programs that empower employees to be advocates during periods of change.

- Communication Strategies: Ensuring clear and transparent communication to facilitate smooth transitions.

Learning and Development:

- Training Programs: Offering targeted training initiatives to enhance employee skills.

- Continuous Learning Culture: Encouraging a culture of continuous learning and development.

- Knowledge Transfer: Facilitating critical knowledge transfer to ensure organizational resilience.

Employee-Centric Approach:

- Self-Service Portals: Empowering employees with self-service tools for HR transactions.

- User-Centered Design: Applying user-centered design principles to HR processes for a more intuitive experience.

- Employee Feedback: Actively seeking and incorporating employee feedback into HR initiatives.

HR Technology Integration:

- Automation of Tasks: Leveraging technology to automate routine and time-consuming HR tasks.

- Data Analytics: Utilizing HR analytics for data-driven decision-making and insights.

- Innovative Tools: Adopting innovative HR technology solutions to enhance efficiency.

Legal and Ethical Compliance:

- Legal Adherence: Ensuring HR practices align with local and international labor laws.

- Ethical Practices: Promoting ethical behavior and ensuring HR policies adhere to ethical standards.

- Risk Management: Mitigating legal and ethical risks associated with HR processes.

Additionally, HR serves as a trusted advisor to senior leaders, providing valuable insights into human capital trends, labor market dynamics, and industry best practices. The following are a few considerations for HR professionals to become true business partners to the company management:

2.1 - Optimize HR Strategies to Support Strategic Objectives

To drive organizational success, it is essential for HR to seamlessly align its goals with the strategic initiatives of the company. HR should maintain proactive and regular communication with senior leaders and key stakeholders to understand the company's business direction. This includes attending strategy meetings, participating in cross-functional discussions, and seeking input from leaders across different departments. It is of utmost importance to comprehend the overarching goals and prioritize their consideration when planning and setting HR goals.

Additionally, HR should proactively identify opportunities for collaboration with other key functions and establish cross-functional teams to drive key initiatives. For example, by partnering with finance on HR program budgeting, collaborating with marketing on employer branding strategies, and working with operations to enhance safety and wellness programs, HR can effectively integrate its efforts with other business functions. This collaboration allows HR to leverage the expertise and resources of these departments, resulting in more effective and cohesive strategies that support the organization's overall objectives. Thus, it is through such strategic endeavors that HR serves as a catalyst in converting the company's vision into tangible achievements.

2.2 - Embrace HR Technology Solutions

By embracing technology, organizations can enhance their HR. Adopting specialized tech solutions like Applicant Tracking Systems, HRIS platforms, and learning management systems enables HR to optimize efficiency, streamline processes, and automate routine tasks. This allows HR professionals to redirect their time and resources towards other strategic initiatives at the organizational level.

Furthermore, HR technology solutions provide accurate and reliable data, allowing HR to take a data-driven approach to decision-making. By analyzing HR metrics, such as employee engagement levels, turnover rates, and diversity statistics, HR can gain insights into the workforce and provide valuable recommendations for relevant organizational strategies. This data-driven approach helps to optimize workforce demographics, address skill gaps, and allocate resources effectively, leading to improved business outcomes.

2.3 - Focus on Building Strong Employee Relationships

HR professionals must cultivate robust connections with employees to serve as trusted partners. By being accessible, responsive, and supportive, HR leaders can establish credibility. This can be done by:

2.3.1- Approachability and Empathy in HR Practices

HR executives should nurture a friendly and accessible demeanor. Implementing an open-door policy that welcomes employees to seek HR guidance and support with ease is essential. When employees encounter challenges or difficulties, HR should respond promptly and empathetically, showcasing a genuine understanding of their concerns.

Create a secure environment for open dialogue where emotions are acknowledged and validated. This enables them to voice their concerns with no fear of negative consequences.

Ensure strict confidentiality when employees share personal or sensitive information, assuring them that their concerns will be handled with complete respect for their privacy.

Serve as a mediator in impartially addressing conflicts or disputes that may arise inside the organization. Implement an unbiased resolution process that ensures all involved parties are given the opportunity to be heard and respected.

2.3.2 - Nurture Personal Engagement

Initiate regular check-ins through periodic emails or face to face meetings with employees to assess their satisfaction, address any concerns, and provide assistance if necessary. Helping employees identify growth opportunities, facilitating resources for skill enhancement, and advocating for their career advancement is important. Proactively reaching out to them showcases a commitment to their growth and wellness.

Invest efforts and time to establish personal connections with employees. Use their names, explore their passions and hobbies, and display a sincere interest in their lives. Utilize different avenues for staying connected with employees on a personal level such as customized newsletters, birthday greetings, or even a company-wide platform where employees can share personal achievements and interests.

Acknowledge and celebrate employee milestones and achievements. This could include work anniversaries, project successes, or professional certifications. Personalized recognition fosters a sense of appreciation and reinforces the idea that each employee's contributions are valued. Building personal connections fosters trust and strengthens the relationship between employees and HR.

2.3.3 - Improve based on Employee Feedback

Consistently pursue opportunities to enhance HR practices by actively seeking employee feedback and adapting to their evolving needs. One powerful strategy involves implementing regular pulse surveys or feedback sessions tailored to various aspects of the employee experience. By delving into the granular details of their day-to-day interactions with HR processes, organizations can uncover nuanced insights that might otherwise go unnoticed. These surveys should not only focus on identifying pain points but also on recognizing successful practices that contribute positively to the workplace.

Furthermore, creating a dedicated feedback platform ensures that employees can easily share their perspectives, contributing to a culture of open communication. This can be augmented by leveraging modern communication tools, such as collaboration platforms, idea forums, or anonymous suggestion boxes, allowing employees to express their thoughts freely. By doing so, HR departments can tap into the diverse voices gaining a comprehensive understanding of the collective sentiment.

Beyond conventional feedback mechanisms, fostering a culture of continuous improvement involves the active participation of HR personnel in cross-functional collaboration.

Establishing interdisciplinary task forces or committees that include representatives from various departments ensures a holistic approach to process enhancement. This enriches the feedback collection process and also encourages a sense of ownership among employees as they witness the tangible outcomes of their suggestions.

To truly stand out, organizations can also explore innovative methods such as gamification to encourage active participation in the feedback process. By turning the feedback mechanism into an interactive and rewarding experience, employees are more likely to contribute consistently and feel a deeper connection to the improvement initiatives.

Furthermore, to create a secure environment for open dialogue, consider implementing confidential "listening sessions" where employees can share their thoughts and concerns anonymously. This additional layer of privacy encourages a more candid expression of sentiments, providing HR with unfiltered insights into the real challenges employees face. The data gathered from such sessions can then be used to inform targeted HR initiatives that directly address the identified pain points.

2.3.4 - Showcase Transparency and Honesty

Transparency is paramount in this transformative journey. Effectively communicate the specifics of organizational changes, policies, and decisions, along with comprehensive explanations for their underlying rationale. This fosters a sense of inclusion among employees and also provides them with valuable insights into the decision-making process. Furthermore, maintaining thorough documentation of policies, procedures, and decisions such that all employees can easily access the information.

HR professionals should also meticulously document the actions taken in response of employee suggestions. Implementing a comprehensive reporting system that details the changes made based on feedback fosters trust and demonstrates the organization's commitment to employee well-being.

In addition, organizations can consider organizing regular town hall meetings or forums where HR leaders share the results of feedback initiatives and engage in open discussions with employees. This two way communication also acts as a catalyst for further engagement and collaboration with employees.

2.4 - Enhancing Business Acumen

To add value to their organizations, HR professionals should work on gaining a comprehensive understanding of the business landscape and its challenges. By closely monitoring the competitive environment, comprehending the company's financials, and acquiring a comprehensive knowledge of its products or services, HR professionals can offer valuable insights and guidance to senior leaders.

Participating in networking events, and actively seeking continuous learning opportunities empower HR professionals to bring back innovative ideas to their organizations. Keeping abreast of changes in employment law, advancements in HR technologies, and evolving workforce trends is crucial to ensure the relevance and effectiveness of HR practices.

2.5 - Measuring HR's Impact on Business Outcomes

HR professionals must demonstrate the impact of their strategies on business outcomes. Here are some key steps to consider:

2.5.1 - Define Key Metrics

Identifying specific metrics that are integral to HR initiatives and are well aligned with broader business objectives is a vital undertaking, one that requires a deep understanding of how human resources can strategically contribute to the overall success of a company. To illustrate this, let's delve into a hypothetical scenario featuring a software company as our guiding example throughout this section.

In this case, our software company recognized the significance of the "revenue per employee" metric. They understood that to enhance profitability, they needed to focus on both employee productivity and the quality of their work. With this in mind, the HR dept. decided to introduce an employee training program, positioning it as a pivotal initiative to boost their "revenue per employee" metric.

In pursuit of their goal, the HR department meticulously pinpointed several key metrics directly linked to their training program's objectives. These metrics included:

- Software Defect Rate: a metric used in software development. It is a measure of the number of defects, bugs, or issues found in software relative to a specific unit of measurement, often tied to a certain period or a particular quantity of code.
- Lead Time: measures the time it takes from the initiation of a project or feature to its delivery to the end user, helping assess how quickly work is completed.
- Customer Satisfaction Scores: metric used to assess and measure the level of satisfaction or contentment that customers have with a product, service, or overall experience provided by a company.

Each of these metrics was chosen with a precise aim to enhance software quality, elevate employee productivity, and improve the overall customer experience. Ultimately, these improvements were anticipated to contribute to the augmentation of "revenue per employee." Predefined metrics not only provide a well-defined route for monitoring progress but also acts as a robust feedback mechanism.

2.5.2 - Establish Baseline Data and Implement Data Collection Systems

Gather and establish baseline data to understand the current state of the chosen metrics. This provides a benchmark against which progress can be measured over time. For instance, the software development company in our example can start by collecting baseline data on the chosen metrics by:

- Collaborating with the software development and quality assurance teams to access historical defect data.
- Collaborating with project managers and development teams to access project records and review historical project timelines records.
- Aggregating the customer feedback data over a specific timeframe.

The baseline data captures the "before" picture, enabling HR to track and analyze changes over time. Without this crucial step, it would be challenging to quantify the effectiveness of HR initiatives, and strategic decision-making would be a shot in the dark. Establishing such baseline data might also improve the planning and execution of the whole training program.

Moreover, the HR department should establish robust procedures for data collection, ensuring a steady and consistent flow of data for these metrics. This facilitates more profound analysis for future improvements.

2.5.3 - Analyze and Interpret Data

Analyze the data collected both before and after the training to uncover meaningful insights. Seek out recurring trends, patterns, and correlations between HR initiatives and their impact on the relevant metrics/business outcomes. This analytical process serves to pinpoint areas of success and those in need of improvement.

For instance, within the HR team, an observation was made that, following the introduction of the new training program, there was a significant reduction in the number of software defects reported by customers. Remarkably, this decrease in defects coincided with a notable increase in customer satisfaction scores during the same timeframe. By dissecting these patterns and trends, it became evident that the enhanced training program played a direct role in elevating product quality, ultimately leading to heightened customer satisfaction.

However, the analysis also sheds light on a lag in employee productivity, particularly regarding lead time. A deeper investigation, including interviews with participants and other stakeholders, uncovered that the extended duration of the training program might be occupying a substantial portion of participants' productive hours. This data-driven analysis steered them towards informed decisions about refining the program's duration, delivery style, and means to optimize its impact.

2.5.4 - Connect HR Initiatives to Business Outcomes and Communicate Findings Effectively

Prove clear connections between HR initiatives and their impact on specific business outcomes. Quantify the effects whenever possible, highlighting the value of HR strategies to the organization. Effectively communicate the findings with key stakeholders, including senior leaders and executives.

In our example, by meticulously analyzing the data, the HR team found that as the software quality improved, customer satisfaction scores rose by 15%. This increase in customer satisfaction directly translated into a 10% increase in customer retention rates. As a result, customer lifetime value (CLV: CLV represents the predicted net profit generated over the entire relationship with a customer. It's a quantitative measure that estimates the total value a customer will bring to a business throughout their association with that business) increased by 12%.

The HR team quantified the cost savings associated with reduced customer churn and increased CLV, showing that the improved training program resulted in a 20% return on investment (ROI) within the first year of implementation. This data-driven connection demonstrated the value of the HR initiative and its direct impact on key business outcomes.

After analyzing the data, the HR team prepared a presentation that highlighted these findings. It showcased HR's strategic role in achieving these outcomes and provided clear evidence of the measurable impact on the organization's bottom line, making a compelling case for continued investment in employee training programs.

2.5.5 - Continuously Evaluate and Adjust HR Strategies

Consistently evaluate and adapt HR strategies and initiatives based on the insights to enhance their effectiveness on business outcomes and maintain their continuous relevance and accuracy. Following the initial success of their employee training program in our example, the HR team implemented a quarterly review mechanism.

They also periodically conducted surveys among employees to solicit their feedback and gain insights into their preferences/concerns regarding training delivery and content. This iterative approach to evaluation and adjustment guaranteed that HR strategies remained aligned with the company's objectives.

Conclusion

In this chapter we explored the essential elements of fostering high performance within organizations by harnessing the potential of people and culture. Following are the crucial takeaways:

Embrace the Power of High-Performing Individuals

Put emphasis on hiring and developing top class talent who will drive your organization's success. Optimize hiring practices and build a reputed employer brand for the organization.

Develop a Result-Oriented Workforce

Encourage employees to expand their knowledge, embrace new ideas, and constantly seek improvement. Establish an effective performance management system.

Create a Safe and Inclusive Workplace

Strive to build an environment where everyone feels respected, valued, and empowered to contribute their best. Embrace the richness of diverse perspectives, backgrounds, and experiences, and actively promote an inclusive environment where everyone can thrive.

Prioritize Employee Holistic Well-being

Recognize that the well-being of your employees directly affects their performance. Provide resources to support their physical, emotional and mental health.

Align your Culture with Organizational Values

Ensure that your actions, behaviors, and decision-making reflect the values you uphold, creating a cohesive and purpose-driven organization.

Continuously Improve

Consistently evaluate your hiring processes, training programs, and workplace practices to pinpoint opportunities for enhancing organizational culture and refining people strategies.

Prioritize HR

Place a high level of importance on the Human Resources (HR) function within an organization. Elevate the HR department's effectiveness by proactively preparing it to function as a strategic partner, aligning its activities with organizational goals.

Remember, the journey to cultivating high performance begins with a belief in the power of people and a commitment to building a holistically positive culture. This is the key to fostering employee well-being and propelling them toward achieving exceptional results.

Chapter 3 - Cultivating Exceptional Leadership for High-Performance Organizations

Leadership is the catalyst that transforms aspirations into achievements, and organizations into legacies.

Effective leadership plays is pivotal in guiding organizations toward their goals and objectives. This influential force empowers individuals, teams, and the entire organization to tap into their full potential and attain remarkable outcomes. It's crucial to emphasize that leadership isn't confined to particular job titles or positions; it can emerge in anyone showcasing leadership qualities and exemplifying determination. This dynamic inclusiveness highlights that leadership extends beyond conventional boundaries. Now, Let's take a closer look at the factors that contribute to a leader's success and investigate how these leaders play a pivotal role in igniting a culture of excellence within their organizations.

1- Leadership Traits for High-Performance Organizations

The extraordinary ability to inspire and motivate teams to achieve exceptional results characterizes leadership in high-performance organizations. Below are the key attributes that define outstanding leaders in these organizations, shedding light on the qualities and skills that set them apart.

1.1 - Visionary and Strategic Thinking

Visionary leadership is the remarkable ability to transcend current circumstances. It involves perceiving extraordinary possibilities and outcomes that have the potential to surpass the current state of organizational performance. This type of leadership is forward-thinking and innovative, and encourages a transformative approach to achieving success. Visionary thinking entails identifying emerging trends, understanding market dynamics, and anticipating future opportunities and challenges.

Strategic thinking involves analyzing the current situation and formulating a clear and well-defined plan to achieve specific objectives. It encompasses considering multiple factors, evaluating available resources, and aligning actions and decisions with the long-term vision. Thus, it requires leaders to adopt a systematic and thoughtful approach to decision-making, prioritization, and resource allocation.

1.2 - Emotional Intelligence and Empathy

Emotional intelligence encompasses the capacity to recognize, understand, and manage our own emotions while also empathizing with the emotions of others. It involves self-awareness and the ability to regulate our emotions effectively. Additionally, it implies perceiving and comprehending the emotions of those around us, facilitating meaningful communication, collaboration, and relationship building.

Empathy, as a crucial aspect of emotional intelligence, entails not only understanding but also sharing the feelings and perspectives of others. It surpasses mere sympathy or pity, requiring us to genuinely put ourselves in someone else's shoes and establish a deep connection with their emotional experience. By practicing empathy, leaders can respond with care, compassion, and understanding, thereby nurturing positive relationships and fostering effective interpersonal interactions.

1.3 - Resilience and Adaptability

Resilience encompasses the remarkable ability to bounce back and recover from challenges, setbacks, or adversity. It involves maintaining a positive mindset, adapting to change, and effectively coping with stress or challenging circumstances. Resilient leaders possess inner strength and determination to persevere through obstacles and continue moving forward. They embrace failures as learning opportunities, develop strategies to overcome challenges, and sustain their motivation even in difficult situations.

Adaptability is the hallmark of thriving in ever-changing environments or situations. It encompasses the qualities of flexibility and open-mindedness in welcoming new approaches and ideas. Those who embody adaptability possess the remarkable ability to swiftly assess and comprehend diverse circumstances, allowing them to adapt their strategies or behaviors accordingly. They effortlessly navigate through transitions and unexpected changes, exhibiting comfort in the face of uncertainty and a readiness to seize emerging opportunities.

1.4 - Decisiveness and Risk-Taking

Decisiveness refers to the ability to make firm and timely decisions in various situations. It involves assessing available options, considering relevant information, and confidently choosing a course of action. Decisive leaders can weigh the pros and cons, evaluate potential outcomes, and make informed choices without excessive hesitation or indecision, even amidst the ambiguities. They are able to analyze complex situations, gather necessary information, and trust their judgment to arrive at a decisive conclusion.

Risk-taking is the willingness to take calculated risks to pursue goals and opportunities. It involves evaluating the potential risks and rewards associated with a particular course of action and making choices that push boundaries and drive progress. Risk-taking individuals are fearless in stepping outside their comfort zones and exploring new possibilities. They can effectively assess and manage risks, identify potential obstacles, and develop contingency plans. By taking calculated risks, leaders can discover new opportunities, spark innovation, and achieve significant breakthroughs.

1.5 - Effective Communication

Skillful communication is the bedrock of successful interactions, denoting the mastery of conveying information, ideas, thoughts, and emotions with absolute clarity and precision. However, it extends beyond mere message transmission; it involves active listening, empathy, and feedback to foster mutual understanding. Effective communicators possess diverse skills, including verbal and nonverbal techniques like speaking, listening, writing, body language, and visual aids, enabling them to connect and engage proficiently with others.

Mastery of communication empowers leaders to express thoughts and ideas clearly, ensuring resonance with their audience. Moreover, they navigate conflicts and misunderstandings adeptly, cultivating an environment conducive to collaboration and cooperation. Beyond the realm of information sharing, such leaders hold the ability to inspire and motivate. Through the art of storytelling and persuasive language, they possess the power to influence, spurring action and driving significant change.

Adaptive communication is a hallmark of these leaders. They adapt their approach to cater to a diverse range of stakeholders, tailoring messages to resonate effectively with varied audiences. By prioritizing effective communication, leaders unlock a world of opportunities for connection and knowledge exchange in their organizations.

1.6 - Growth Mindset

A growth mindset is not merely a belief system; it is a transformative mindset embracing the notion that abilities, intelligence, and skills can be developed through effort, learning, and practice. Leaders with a growth mindset view challenges, obstacles, and failures as opportunities for personal growth and learning rather than indicators of fixed limitations. This mindset empowers them to approach their work with curiosity, openness, and resilience. Such leaders are more inclined to embrace new experiences and step outside their comfort zones.

1.7 - Trust and Transparency

At the foundation of effective leadership lies the crucial element of trust. For leaders to succeed, they must diligently cultivate and maintain the trust of their team members through the consistent practice of transparency and integrity. Open and authentic communication fosters an environment of psychological safety among employees. Building and preserving trust also requires aligning one's words with actions, demonstrating an unwavering dedication to fulfilling commitments, and exhibiting integrity in every facet of decision-making.

2- Leadership Styles

Effective leadership comes in various forms, each with its unique approach and strengths. Let's explore some key leadership styles that have proven effective in high-performance organizations.

2.1 - Transformational Leadership

Transformational leaders excel in inspiring and motivating teams, placing a strong emphasis on personal growth and development. They invest time in understanding each team member's aspirations and talents, aligning roles with strengths. This tailored approach encourages innovation, fosters extraordinary accomplishments, and promotes a shared commitment to a compelling vision.

Visualize an engineering manager of a tech team in a software company. She invests the time to deeply grasp the strengths and aspirations of her team members. She entrusts a skilled frontend coder (who aspires to master full-stack development) with progressively challenging tasks encompassing both frontend and backend components. This gradual elevation reflects her understanding of the coder's passion and potential.

In tandem, she eloquently articulates and reinforces the company's vision of pioneering transformative software that will reshape the industry landscape. Her communication style captivates her team, fostering a collective commitment to this visionary goal.

Furthermore, she firmly believes in empowering her team to chart their work methodologies autonomously. As a direct result, the team consistently delivers innovative solutions, benefiting from their intrinsic motivation and the manager's trust in their decision-making abilities.

2.2 - Servant Leadership

Servant leaders prioritize team members' needs, actively serving by providing resources, support, and a listening ear. They value well-being and growth, fostering trust and respect. This approach inspires ownership, responsibility, and exceptional performance, strengthening team unity through esteem and motivation.

Picture a school principal who practices servant leadership. He actively listens to his teaching staff and provides them with the necessary resources and support. He values the well-being and growth of each teacher. When a teacher proposes a new teaching method, the principal supports its implementation. His altruistic approach fosters trust and respect among the teachers, leading to a harmonious and high-performing school environment.

2.3 - Situational Leadership

Situational leaders adapt their style to meet their teams' varying needs and circumstances. Recognizing that different situations require different levels of support and direction, they demonstrate flexibility and versatility. This approach maximizes team effectiveness, enhancing performance and dynamics by tailoring leadership to the specific context.

Consider a project manager who employs situational leadership in a marketing agency. She recognizes that some team members are experienced and highly motivated while others are new and need more guidance. For the seasoned team members, she provides autonomy and lets them make decisions. For the newer team members, she offers more guidance and support. This flexible approach ensures that both groups perform optimally, contributing to the project's success

2.4 - Authentic Leadership

Authentic leaders champion genuineness, transparency, and maintaining one's true self. By actively listening, demonstrating empathy, and supporting the team, they foster mutual respect and strong connections. Furthermore, by embodying authenticity, they encourage open communication, thereby establishing emotional security and enhancing teamwork.

Think of a department head in a software company who practices authentic leadership. He openly shares the company's challenges and seeks feedback from his team on how to overcome them. He listens to their concerns and actively supports their professional development. This transparency and empathy create a culture of trust where team members feel comfortable providing input and working together to solve problems.

3 - Cultivating Excellence: Leadership in High-Performance Organizations

Let's explore how a leader nurtures a culture of excellence in the organization:

3.1 - Creating a High-Performance Culture

Instead of relying on rigid policies, governance practices, or excessive micromanagement to extract productivity, cultivating a culture that promotes flexibility and autonomy, empowers both individuals and teams to excel. This culture is driven by values, behaviors, and practices that inspire peak performance. Below, we explore some key practices to build and nurture such a high-performance culture:

3.1.1 - Establish and Communicate Clear Organizational Mission and Values

It is necessary to ensure that the mission and values deeply resonate with every individual in the organization. This aspect is elaborately explained in Chapter 2, 1.3.3 - Building a Culture That Supports Organizational Values

3.1.2 - Create an Inclusive Work Environment

Effective leaders strive to create an inclusive work environment that empowers team members to be their authentic selves and maximize their strengths. This requires proactive steps to prioritize inclusivity in policies, behavior, and culture such as:

- **Implement Inclusive Policies:** Develop and enforce policies that prioritize inclusivity in all aspects of the workplace.

- **Voice your Support:** Actively champion an inclusive culture by expressing support and commitment to diversity.

- **Promote Inclusive Language:** Encourage language that respects and values differences.

- **Listen:** Regularly listen to and validate the perspectives of all team members. Facilitate Transparency: Foster open and candid discussions to create a culture of trust and understanding.

- **Share Updates:** Keep the team informed about diversity and inclusion initiatives, progress, and challenges, emphasizing the organization's dedication to inclusivity.

3.1.3 - Nurturing a Growth Mindset and Fostering Innovation

Nurturing a growth mindset and fostering innovation are key leadership responsibilities. Let's look at some ways to do this:

- **Demonstrate a Growth Mindset:** Show enthusiasm for learning, openly discuss challenges and failures, and prioritize continuous improvement.

- **Provide Constructive Feedback:** Offer feedback that focuses on growth and development, not just performance evaluations.

- **Acknowledge Efforts:** Recognize and value the efforts and progress made by individuals to reinforce the importance of continuous learning.

- **Celebrate Learning Achievements:** Celebrate milestones and learning achievements to emphasize the significance of putting in effort and pursuing ongoing education.

- **Create a Safe Environment:** Establish a safe space where failures are seen as opportunities for growth and improvement.

- **Promote Professional Development:** Offer professional development opportunities, knowledge sharing, and mentorship or coaching relationships.

- **Value Innovation:** Cultivate a culture that values and encourages new ideas, empowering employees to question the status quo.

- **Allocate Resources:** Provide resources and tools to support innovation initiatives and facilitate the exploration of new concepts.

- **Encourage Innovation Initiatives:** Promote innovation through dedicated teams and enable designated time for innovative projects, collaboration, and brainstorming.

3.1.4 - Promote Leadership Development Programs

Promoting leadership development programs is a crucial but often overlooked responsibility of leaders. It involves grooming individuals for leadership roles, whether at the organizational or team level. Effective leadership development entails a combination of following initiatives:

- **Robust Leadership Programs:** Develop comprehensive leadership programs that incorporate formal and informal training.

- **Encourage Participation:** Promote engagement in leadership workshops, conferences, and industry events where individuals can enhance their skills, learn from experts, and collaborate with peers.

- **Tailored Training:** Customize programs to cater to individuals at various career stages, ensuring they receive the appropriate training and guidance.

- **Cross-Functional Collaboration:** Create opportunities for employees to collaborate on cross-functional projects, providing exposure to different aspects of the business and fostering a holistic understanding of leadership.

- **Invest in Future Leaders:** Leaders who invest in these initiatives not only build a pipeline of potential future leaders but also foster a culture of continuous learning.

3.2 - Leading for High Performance in Challenging Situations

Leading in challenging and uncertain situations, especially during times of crisis, presents unique difficulties for leaders. The heightened sense of urgency, increased pressure, and the need for swift decision-making can be overwhelming. Leaders must navigate uncharted territory, making tough choices with limited information and resources.

They face the challenge of managing their emotions and fears while providing guidance and reassurance to their teams. Here are critical insights into how leading in challenging times differs from leading in regular times:

3.2.1 - Navigate Ambiguity with Proactive Decision-Making

Navigating ambiguity with proactive decision-making is a critical leadership skill when faced with situations characterized by limited information and unclear paths. It empowers leaders to overcome challenges stemming from uncertainty and ensures that progress remains unhindered by indecisiveness.

- **Gather Diverse Perspectives:** Seek input from individuals with varying expertise and viewpoints, fostering open and honest discussions to uncover valuable insights and alternative views.

- **Prioritize Essential Information:** Identify critical data required for informed decisions and focus on gathering relevant information while avoiding unnecessary data that may lead to analysis paralysis.

- **Maintain a Long-Term Focus:** Balance the need for immediate attention and agility with a commitment to the organization's mission, vision, and strategic goals. Ensure that decisions align with long-term objectives, providing stability and direction even in the face of short-term challenges.

- **Assess Risks and Benefits:** Evaluate potential risks and benefits of various options, considering short-term and long-term implications. Avoid impulsive reactions, opt for a measured approach, and base decisions on available data and potential consequences.

- **Develop Decision-Making Frameworks:** Establish structured decision-making frameworks or guidelines that consider factors the impact, feasibility, and alignment with organizational goals.

- **Continuously Reassess and Course-Correct:** Regularly review decisions and their effectiveness. Be prepared to adjust course if new information/circumstances call for a different approach.

3.2.2 - Prioritize Communication

Leaders must communicate frequently, clearly, and transparently during challenging times. While you may not have all the answers, it is always beneficial to acknowledge uncertainty, share what is known at the time, and provide context and rationale behind decisions being made.

Schedule regular team meetings, town halls, or virtual check-ins to share important information and address any questions or concerns. This allows for direct communication and enables team members to seek clarification. By keeping the lines of communication open during such times, leaders can foster trust, alleviate anxiety, and keep their teams engaged.

3.2.3 - Prioritize Employee Well-being

Leaders must show heightened empathy to prioritize employee well-being, particularly during challenging times. They need to stay approachable for their teams, offering guidance and reassurance. It's important to acknowledge the emotional challenges individuals may face in such difficult circumstances.

Also, they must reinforce the importance of self-care from time to time within their teams. Ensuring that employees have access to resources and support systems such as Employee

Assistance Programs (EAPs), counseling services, or workshops focused on stress management and resilience can assist them in navigating challenging circumstances.

3.2.4 - Involve Employees

Leaders must create an environment where individuals can collaborate, share ideas, and work collectively to find solutions for challenging problems. They can encourage collaboration by facilitating team discussions, brainstorming sessions, and cross-functional projects. Good leaders navigate difficulties effectively by tapping into their teams' collective intelligence and creativity.

3.2.5 – Exemplify Ideal Behavior

Leaders must demonstrate the behaviors they expect from their teams during difficult times. As such, they can show resilience by maintaining a positive attitude and staying calm under pressure. They can openly share their experiences of overcoming challenges and highlight the lessons learned from setbacks. By modeling the desired behaviors, leaders inspire their teams to emulate them and maintain a high-performance mindset.

3.3 - Building and Developing High-Performance Teams

Effective leadership involves assembling and nurturing teams that consistently deliver exceptional results. To achieve this, managers and team leaders must adopt a strategic and intentional approach, considering key factors contributing to team success and the nuances of team dynamics. Here are insights and considerations for this process:

3.3.1 - Set Effective Goals for Individual and Organizational Success

Leaders play a crucial role in setting goals that drive both individual and organizational success. It is of fundamental importance to align personal and team goals with the organization's vision, providing clarity and direction on how each employee's work contributes to the overall success. Confirm that each team member clearly understands their roles and responsibilities.

Involving employees in the goal-setting process ensures goals are realistic and attainable. Provide opportunities for employees to provide input, discuss their aspirations, and identify meaningful goals for them and the organization.

Clearly define what needs to be accomplished, how progress will be measured, and the timeline for achieving the goals. This clarity helps employees focus their efforts and track their progress effectively. Regularly review progress toward goals, provide constructive feedback, and offer guidance and support to help employees stay on track.

3.3.2 - Promote Collaboration and Knowledge Sharing

Collaboration should extend beyond team boundaries and encompass cross-functional collaboration. Strategically assign members from diverse teams or departments to collaborate on projects. Utilize digital tools, such as project management software and communication platforms, to facilitate seamless partnerships and effortless information sharing.

Initiate regular knowledge-sharing sessions, such as workshops or webinars, to provide opportunities for team members to exchange expertise and best practices. Actively participate in these initiatives and create a safe space for idea sharing and feedback. We will study the significance of a knowledge-sharing culture and its practical implementation in Chapter 7.

3.3.3 - Nurture the Personal and Professional Growth

Apart from advocating and facilitating their training programs and regular learning, leaders can significantly affect their team members ' growth by openly sharing their knowledge and experience. Conducting coaching sessions along with regular feedback can affect the team's overall growth. Assigning challenging projects that stretch their capabilities and diligently putting efforts into their development planning is also crucial.

Moreover, a good leader goes beyond focusing solely on professional growth. They also recognize the importance of personal growth and actively support their team members in achieving this. Remember that a person's attitude, mindset, and personal qualities can be just as influential as their technical skills in determining their success as an employee.

3.3.4 - Recognize and Celebrate Individual and Team Achievements

Show appreciation for individual and team accomplishments through diverse methods, including public recognition, rewards, and avenues for growth and advancement. Leaders should also encourage peer-to-peer recognition, where team members regularly appreciate and celebrate each other's accomplishments.

3.3.5 - Encourage Autonomy and Ownership

It involves trusting your team members to make decisions and take responsibility for their work. To support this, leaders should ensure that team members have the resources to carry out their duties effectively. It's important to provide clear guidelines and expectations for assigned tasks. Guidance can be offered as needed, but it's equally important to allow flexibility. This will enable individuals to approach the work in their own way and find independent solutions. This also creates a space for learning from mistakes and promotes resiliency.

3.3.6 - Prioritize Work-Life Balance and Cultivate Resiliency Within Team

Leaders and managers can play a crucial role in prioritizing work-life balance within their spheres of influence. While organizational policies may endorse this balance, its success depends on team dynamics and protocols. Creating an environment that champions work-life balance is a vital responsibility for leaders and managers.

- **Encourage Open Discussions:** Foster open team discussions about workload, stress management, and personal well-being. Create a safe space for team members to voice their concerns.

- **Set Clear Boundaries:** Demonstrate your commitment by setting clear boundaries and integrating a healthy work-life balance. Avoid excessive overtime and encourage team members to take time off for rejuvenation.

- **Provide Flexibility:** Offer flexibility in work arrangements whenever possible to create an environment where individuals can thrive personally and professionally.

- **Open Conversations About Well-being:** Encourage open conversations about well-being, making team members comfortable discussing challenges and seeking help when needed.

- **Share Experiences:** As a leader, share your own experiences and coping strategies to create a sense of vulnerability and empathy within the team.

- **Regular Well-being Assessment:** Continuously assess the well-being of team members and take proactive measures to address signs of burnout or excessive stress. Adjust workloads, provide support, or consider flexible work arrangements as necessary.

- **Invest in Resilience Programs:** Allocate resources to development programs focusing on building psychological resilience. These programs should enhance coping mechanisms, stress management skills, and emotional strength, equipping the team to navigate challenges, recover from setbacks, and maintain high performance.

3.3.7 - Continuously Refine Team Dynamics

A leader must evaluate and enhance how team members interact, communicate, and collaborate. This involves addressing factors affecting team efficiency, such as communication styles, decision-making methods, conflict-resolution strategies, and teamwork. These refinements can lead to improved team performance. Evaluate how team members work together, identify any areas of inefficiency or conflict, and understand the strengths and weaknesses of the team as a first step towards improving the internal dynamics.

Facilitate regular team meetings or discussions to address challenges or disputes and find collaborative solutions. Offering training and development opportunities can improve interpersonal skills and encourage successful teamwork. This may involve organizing workshops focused on communication, conflict resolution, or team-building activities that foster trust and cooperation.

3.4 - Insights for Enhancing Performance in Distributed Teams:

Building a high-performing distributed team adds an additional layer of complexity to team management. Here are some specific insights:

3.4.1 - Provide Clear Guidelines and Processes for Remote Work

Establishing well-defined guidelines is crucial for enhancing clarity and effectiveness within a distributed team. These guidelines enable remote team members to work independently while staying aligned with the team's objectives.

- **Communication Protocols:** Develop clear communication protocols outlining expectations for stand-ups, virtual meetings, check-in frequencies, response times, and preferred communication channels to accommodate diverse time zones and working preferences.

- **Prioritize Transparency:** Emphasize transparency and open communication by promptly sharing vital updates, documents, and resources with all team members.

- **Enhance Meeting Engagement:** Encourage active participation and engagement in virtual meetings by providing clear agendas and allowing space for all team members to contribute their ideas and perspectives.

- **Promote Active Listening:** Foster active listening and empathy to overcome misunderstandings and build stronger interpersonal connections.

- **Task Management Guidelines:** Set clear task management guidelines, including deadlines, deliverables, and progress tracking, to ensure accountability and productivity.

- **Knowledge Sharing:** Enhance collaboration by introducing knowledge-sharing and documentation guidelines, facilitating easy access to critical information and expertise, thus reducing knowledge gaps.

- **Transparent Decision-Making:** Implement transparent decision-making processes that outline roles and responsibilities, decision criteria, and escalation procedures, ensuring clarity in responsibilities and promoting efficient decision-making.

3.4.2 - Foster a Sense of Belonging and Build Rapport

To foster a sense of belonging among team members, leaders must proactively create opportunities for connection and engagement. This is especially crucial in distributed teams where physical proximity is limited.

- **Facilitate Belongingness:** Actively create platforms or channels for remote team members to engage in non-work-related conversations and form social bonds.

- **Promote Social Interaction:** Encourage virtual coffee breaks, informal chats, or team-building activities to foster camaraderie and connection among team members.

- **Embrace Diversity and Inclusion:** Recognize the significance of diversity and inclusion within distributed teams. Celebrate the unique perspectives, backgrounds, and experiences of each team member.

- **Regular One-on-One Meetings:** Arrange regular one-on-one meetings with team members to discuss their progress, challenges, and goals. Use this time to build rapport, offer guidance, and address concerns.

- **Video Calls for Personal Connection:** Opt for video calls over audio or text messages whenever possible to establish a more personal connection and build trust.

- **Keep the Team Informed:** Keep the team informed about important company updates, changes, and milestones to maintain transparency.

- **Acknowledge Achievements:** Publicly acknowledge and appreciate individual and team achievements during meetings or through company-wide communication channels. Celebrate milestones and successes to boost morale and strengthen the team's positive culture.

3.4.3 - Leverage technology

Leveraging technology effectively is a critical requirement for the success of distributed teams. It enables seamless communication, collaboration, and access to essential resources, regardless of team members' locations.

- **Utilize Collaboration Tools:** Implement collaboration tools and technologies to facilitate communication and collaboration among remote teams. Video conferencing and instant messaging provide real-time communication, feedback, and decision-making, reducing communication barriers.

- **Invest in Project Management Software:** Support efficient teamwork by investing in project management software, virtual whiteboards, and document-sharing platforms. These tools enable real-time collaboration and ensure access to essential information and resources.

- **Embrace Cloud-Based Tools:** Utilize cloud-based tools and digital platforms that empower remote team members to access work-related documents, files, and resources from anywhere. This enhances collaboration on projects, progress tracking, and resource allocation, resulting in increased productivity and efficiency.

Conclusion

Exemplary leadership not only catalyzes peak performance in stable conditions but also equips organizations to navigate and flourish amidst change and adversity. The cornerstone of achieving outstanding performance is bringing together individuals with diverse backgrounds, skills, and perspectives in a way that harnesses the collective power of their differences to create a cooperative and harmonious team dynamic. By integrating the insights outlined above, managers and team leaders can nurture a dynamic team culture that, in turn, yields exceptional outcomes.

◆◆◆

Case Study

Satya Nadella: Pioneering Microsoft's Transformation

Satya Nadella's tenure as CEO of Microsoft has been defined by visionary leadership and strategic decision-making. Widely acknowledged as an authentic and transformational leader, Nadella has garnered trust and commitment from employees through his transparency, emotional intelligence, moral grounding, and responsiveness to their needs. His management philosophy centers around growth mindset, focusing deliberately on empathy and individual empowerment.

During Nadella's leadership, Microsoft has undergone significant changes. The company shifted away from proprietary phone hardware and operating systems, embracing subscription-based products with recurring revenue as the core of its business. With a strong emphasis on cloud computing, artificial intelligence (AI), and social networking, Microsoft has become more innovative, collaborative, and customer-focused. Additionally, his proactive acquisition strategy has seen Microsoft invest in companies of varying sizes and diverse strengths, further driving the company's growth and evolution.

Accelerating Transformation Through Visionary Leadership

Microsoft has transformed its cloud business under Nadella's leadership. He took a risk by reducing the prioritization of Windows and Office to make the cloud more of a priority. Still, it paid off, propelling the company to compete with industry giants like Amazon Web Services (AWS). Nadella's cloud-first model has driven massive growth and profitability for partners. He led the development of Microsoft's cloud computing platforms, including Microsoft Azure and Microsoft Dynamics 365. This transformation has been vital to Microsoft's success in recent years.

In the fourth quarter of fiscal year 2021 3.1, Microsoft witnessed a remarkable 36% year-over-year increase in commercial cloud revenue, reaching an impressive $19.5 billion. Azure revenue experienced substantial growth during the same period, surging by 51% in constant currency.

This upward trend persisted into 2022 3.2, as Microsoft reported a 20% increase in cloud revenue to $51.7 billion for the second quarter of fiscal year 2022. Furthermore, in the fourth quarter 3.3 of the same fiscal year, Microsoft's cloud revenue rose by 12% to reach an astounding $51.9 billion.

A pivotal visionary decision was the acquisition of LinkedIn in 2016. Seamlessly merging LinkedIn's offerings with Microsoft's suite of products revolutionized productivity and brought new collaborative advantages. Examples include the fusion of LinkedIn's Sales Navigator with Microsoft Dynamics sales software and the integration of LinkedIn profiles with Office applications.

Nadella's commitment to investing in AI led to the development of powerful tools for developers to build AI-powered applications. The Microsoft AI platform includes pre-trained AI services like Cognitive Services and Bot Framework and deep learning tools like Azure Machine Learning, Visual Studio Code Tools for AI, and Cognitive Toolkit.

Microsoft Cognitive Services is a collection of intelligent APIs that allow systems to see, hear, speak, understand and interpret human needs using natural methods of communication. Developers can use these APIs to make their applications across platforms more intelligent, engaging and discoverable. These services are developed by the Microsoft AI and Research team and expose the latest deep learning algorithms.

Satya believes that AI will continue to be a growth area for the company, driving 'the next major wave of computing'. The partnership with OpenAI drove substantial investments, facilitating further AI research and integrating advanced models into Microsoft's products and services. It also enhanced and powered innovative AI products like GitHub Copilot, DALL·E and ChatGPT. This collaboration has introduced large-scale AI as a powerful, general-purpose technology platform that can create a transformative impact at the magnitude of the personal computer, the internet, mobile devices, and the cloud. This partnership with OpenAI has put Microsoft at the forefront of the tech world's AI race.

Similarly, embracing open-source software marked a significant shift under Nadella's leadership. Microsoft actively embraced open-source technologies, supporting and contributing to projects like GitHub, .NET Core, and Visual Studio Code, fostering collaboration and innovation.

Focus on Inclusive Culture

Under the leadership of Satya Nadella, Microsoft has launched various initiatives to promote inclusion and transparency. A significant commitment is the company's pledge to invest an additional $150 million 0 in diversity inclusion efforts, with the aim of doubling the representation of Black and African American and Hispanic and Latinx people in managerial and leadership positions in the U.S. by 2025. This exemplifies Microsoft's dedication to driving meaningful change.

Microsoft is also evolving its engagement with its supply chain, banking partners, and partner ecosystem. The company recognizes that a stronger and more productive ecosystem requires a better representation of the diversity in our communities.

Furthermore, Microsoft is committed to strengthening communities by using data, technology, and partnerships to help address racial injustice and inequities faced by the

Black and African American communities in the U.S. The objective is to enhance the safety and welfare of both their employees and the communities they serve.

Microsoft transparently releases its Diversity and Inclusion Report annually, showcasing achievements and potential areas for improvement. This report underscores the company's commitment to fostering a diverse and inclusive environment.

In addition, Microsoft actively collaborates with minority- and women-owned businesses, invests in developing future tech industry leaders, and seeks candidates from diverse backgrounds to support their success. These initiatives highlight Microsoft's strategic approach to diversity and inclusion.

Exemplary Commitment to Sustainability

Microsoft has demonstrated a steadfast dedication to sustainability and combating climate change under Nadella's guidance. In 2020, the company announced ambitious targets to achieve carbon-negative status by 2030 and eliminate all historical carbon emissions by 2050 3.5. To achieve these sustainability goals, Microsoft has implemented various initiatives focusing on carbon reduction, water conservation, waste management, and biodiversity preservation. Grounded in a principled approach, the company leverages science and mathematics to take responsibility for its carbon footprint and seriously invests in carbon reduction and removal technology.

Microsoft also extends its commitment to sustainability beyond its own operations by empowering customers worldwide, ensuring transparency, advocating for carbon-related public policy issues, and engaging employees in sustainability initiatives. Microsoft Cloud for Sustainability is a set of capabilities and solutions that help organizations accelerate their sustainability progress and business growth. It helps organizations unify data intelligence, build a sustainable IT infrastructure, reduce the environmental impact of operations, and create sustainable value chains.

Some of the features of Microsoft Cloud for Sustainability are:

- **Microsoft Sustainability Manager:** A tool for organizations to track emissions, report progress in real time, and collaborate on sustainability initiatives to transform their business comprehensively.

- **Emissions Impact Dashboard:** A Power BI application that helps Azure enterprise customers estimate and track their carbon emissions and savings related to their cloud usage.

- **Microsoft Cloud for Sustainability API:** This gives the users transparency on the carbon emissions generated by your usage of Azure and Microsoft 365.

- **Industry-specific solutions:** Solutions from Microsoft partners that address the sustainability challenges and opportunities in different sectors, such as manufacturing, retail, energy, and transportation.

Growth Mindset and Customer Focus

Nadella's emphasis on a growth mindset has been instrumental in driving significant transformation. He established a foundation of psychological safety, enabling individuals to extract insights from past failures and convert them into valuable lessons. Concurrently, he nurtured a culture of openness, urging employees to candidly share their mistakes and the lessons learned from them. This shift in emphasis aimed to recognize their efforts, not just fixate on outcomes.

Under his guidance, employees were encouraged to adopt a "learn-it-all" mindset, shedding the limitations of a "know-it-all" attitude, and embracing qualities like curiosity, humility, and open-mindedness. He further motivated them to acquire new skills and stay current with emerging technologies, offering an array of resources and programs to facilitate their learning journey. Nadella's leadership extended to organizational restructuring, effectively dismantling silos and facilitating more seamless cross-functional teamwork and innovation.

At the core of Microsoft's success lies Nadella's commitment to customer focus. He emphasizes understanding customer needs, seeking feedback, and prioritizing their satisfaction. This approach has guided the development of solutions that address customer pain points and deliver value.

The "people-centric IT" approach underscores Microsoft's commitment to providing seamless experiences for customers while meeting their unique needs. Balancing user preferences and IT requirements, Microsoft delivers products and services prioritizing the end-user experience, further solidifying its customer-centric focus.

Overall, Satya Nadella's exemplary leadership has not only transformed Microsoft as a company but has also set a standard for innovation and responsible business practices. His strategic vision, commitment to building a positive culture, and focus on customer satisfaction have left an indelible mark on the organization, inspiring growth and success for years to come.

◆◆◆

Chapter 4 - Change Management for Success

Change is the wind of progress; to navigate it is to chart a course for success.

Embracing change and strategically adapting to it empowers organizations to proactively address market trends and capitalize on emerging opportunities. By fostering a culture that values adaptation, businesses can ensure that they are not only responsive to industry shifts but also pioneers in innovation. The flexibility to evolve enables organizations to optimize processes, enhance efficiency, and cultivate a dynamic workforce. Embracing change is therefore essential for creating a foundation for sustained success.

Mastering the art of navigating change is a key characteristic of a High-Performance Organization (HPO), requiring a methodical approach to planning, executing, and overseeing organizational changes. A well-defined tailored strategy for implementing change can serve as an effective guide for individuals, teams, and the entire organization, facilitating a smooth transition toward the envisioned future state while minimizing resistance and managing risks.

While embracing change offers significant benefits, organizations often encounter hurdles due to various factors. One primary challenge is the fear of the unknown. Change brings uncertainty, and individuals within an organization might be resistant to stepping outside their comfort zones. This resistance can stem from a lack of understanding about the benefits of the proposed changes or a fear of potential disruptions to established routines.

Moreover, organizational inertia can play a significant role. Long-standing processes, structures, and cultures may create a sense of stability, making it difficult for organizations to envision and implement new strategies. The "we've always done it this way" mentality can impede innovation and hinder the adoption of change, even when it is necessary for staying competitive.

Additionally, a lack of effective communication and involvement in the decision-making process can contribute to resistance. If employees feel that changes are imposed without their input or understanding, it can lead to skepticism and pushback. In tandem, organizational leaders wield significant influence in establishing the atmosphere for change adoption. Lack of alignment or a visible commitment to change on the part of leadership can create confusion and undermine efforts to implement new strategies.

It is important to understand that organizational change reverberates beyond systems and structures to affect its people as well. Thus, it places a premium on managing the human aspect of change, encompassing an understanding of and response to the emotions, concerns, and reactions of those affected. This approach underscores the importance of clear communication, stakeholder engagement, and provision of support to aid individuals through the change.

In the absence of a well-structured plan, unclear communication regarding changes can cause confusion, reduced productivity, and a rupture of trust among the organization's members. Moreover, inadequate change management can breed incoherence and disharmony across various departments and teams. A closer examination of the distinct types of changes and their specific objectives is essential to gain a comprehensive understanding of change management. Let's delve into these:

Incremental Change

Incremental change is characterized by the implementation of minor, gradual modifications to current processes, structures, or strategies. This approach is often applied to refine operational methods and address specific inefficiencies / bottleneck. As a result, incremental change maintains a narrow focus and is guided by the goal of steadily enhancing organizational performance.

Transformational Change

Transformational change signifies a major shift reverberating throughout the organization. The ultimate objective of this type of change is to bring about a radical transformation in various aspects, including the organization's structure, culture, processes, and strategies. This type of change is often instigated by external factors such as disruptive technologies, shifts in the market landscape, or industry-wide transformations. Given its far-reaching implications, transformational change demands a substantial dedication of resources, time, and effort to facilitate enduring organizational evolution.

Strategic Change

Strategic change focuses on adjusting an organization's strategic direction and initiatives to adapt to internal or external circumstances. It aims to improve the organization's competitive position, capitalize on emerging opportunities, or address challenges. The scope of strategic change can vary, but it generally involves specific areas of the organization's strategy. This change may involve:

- Redefining goals.
- Repositioning in the market.
- Diversifying product or service offerings.
- Revising the business model.

Technological Change

Technological change encompasses adopting, implementing, or integrating novel organizational technologies. This type of change is geared towards amplifying productivity and innovation. It includes a wide array of initiatives like:

- Implementation of fresh software systems to process automation.
- The embrace of artificial intelligence.
- The digitization of operations

The pace and scope of technological change are determined by the specific technologies introduced and how they permeate various dimensions of the organization.

Cultural Change

Cultural change revolves around reshaping an organization's values, beliefs, behaviors, and norms. Its ultimate goal is cultivating a fresh culture that aligns with sought-after objectives like innovation, collaboration, diversity, and customer-centricity. Cultural change often becomes imperative to facilitate the success of other organizational shifts.

This type of transformation typically demands sustained and long-term efforts. It encompasses various endeavors, such as leadership development, programs to enhance employee engagement, and revisions to reward systems. The impact of cultural change spans across the entire organization and necessitates involvement at every tier.

Structural Change

Structural change involves modifying the organization's formal hierarchy, reporting relationships, processes, or roles and responsibilities. It aims to optimize the organizational structure to better align with strategic objectives or changing market conditions. This change may include:

- Reorganizing departments.
- Merging or splitting business units.
- Decentralizing decision-making.
- Implementing new governance mechanisms.

The scope of structural change varies depending on the extent of the restructuring and its impact on different parts of the organization.

Thus, these different kinds of changes serve distinct purposes, have varying scopes, and are driven by various factors. Organizations may need to implement a combination of these changes to adapt, thrive, and remain competitive.

1 - Factors that Influence Change

Understanding the diverse factors influencing or driving change enables organizations to navigate the forthcoming transformations effectively. This comprehension empowers leaders and decision-makers to formulate robust strategies, optimize resource allocation, and execute focused, ultimately strengthening its competitive stance. Let's study them:

1.1 - External Factors

External factors are influential drivers of organizational change. They encompass elements outside the organization's immediate control that necessitate adaptation and strategic responses. These factors include:

- **Technological Advancements:** The rapid progression of technology, such as AI, IoT, and blockchain, can reshape industries, creating new opportunities and necessitating changes to remain competitive.

- **Intense Competition:** Operating within highly competitive landscapes amidst disruptive business models, new entrants, and shifting market dynamics requires vigilance and adaptability.

- **Evolving Customer Needs:** Adapting to changing customer preferences and market requirements necessitates change in organizational strategies.

- **Global Economic Trends:** Fluctuations in the broader economy including factors like interest rates and economic conditions affects cost management and growth decisions.

- **Regulatory Changes:** Modifications in laws and regulations requires necessary adjustments to organizational processes and practices to ensure compliance with evolving legal requirements.

1.2 - Internal Factors

Internal factors originate within the organization and significantly impact the necessity and direction of change efforts. They include:

- **Leadership Changes:** Transitions in top management positions bring about shifts in the organization's direction and strategies.

- **Workforce Demographics:** The composition of the employee base, including age and diversity can influence HR policies and practices.

- **Organizational Performance:** Organizational performance serves as a pivotal factor driving change, as assessments of efficiency, effectiveness, and key metrics (such as market share, profitability etc.) often highlight areas for improvement and innovation within the company.

- **Inefficiencies:** The proactive identification and rectification of operational bottlenecks, outdated processes, and inefficiencies demands targeted changes to enhance productivity and reduce costs.

- **Financial Changes:** These involve addressing financial constraints through strategic measures, such as restructuring, optimizing resources, or exploring new revenue streams, all aimed at ensuring stability and fostering growth.

- **Growth or Expansion:** Effectively navigating change during periods of growth - whether through market expansion, mergers, acquisitions, or substantial development - demands a structured approach to capitalize on opportunities.

- **Continuous Improvement:** Embracing change to improve workflows, procedures, systems, and culture to enhance operations, efficiency, and customer value in a dynamic and competitive landscape.

2 - Successfully implementing the Change Management

Effective change management requires a systematic approach that empowers HPOs to manage change effectively. Let's look at how an organization can achieve this:

2.1 - Identify the Need for Change

Organizations must recognize and understand the drivers that necessitate adaptation and innovation. Let's explore the ways:

2.1.1 - Holistic Environmental Analysis

Employ a comprehensive approach that seamlessly integrates continuous monitoring and environmental scanning, drawing insights from both internal and external sources. This approach entails the consistent observation and analysis of a multitude of factors, including market trends, technological progress, customer input, regulatory shifts, industry benchmarks, and competitive landscapes. This comprehensive perspective empowers organizations to adeptly recognize change opportunities and make informed decisions grounded in a thorough understanding of the business landscape.

2.1.2 - Internal Assessment

Conduct internal assessments to pinpoint inefficiencies through process audits, performance evaluations, or employee feedback sessions. Encourage open and honest communication to gather insights into areas that require change and improvement within the organization.

2.1.3 - Data Analysis

Harnessing the potential of data analytics offers a potent and efficient avenue to extract valuable insights from extensive datasets. Enterprises can heighten their decision-making prowess by dissecting customer behavior, sales records, operational metrics, and pertinent data reservoirs. Through this process, organizations can unveil intricate patterns and emerging trends that may signal the need for strategic or operational adjustments. Relying on such data-driven insights amplifies precision and impartiality in recognizing areas for improvement.

2.1.4 - Stakeholder Engagement

Engage with stakeholders at various levels, including employees, customers, suppliers, and industry experts. Solicit their input on current challenges and the necessity for optimizations. This can be done through structured feedback mechanisms such as surveys, focus groups or interviews.

2.1.5 - Cross-Functional Collaboration

Establish cross-functional teams or task forces that bring together individuals from different teams, departments, or expertise. This collaborative approach allows for a holistic view of the organization and facilitates the identification of interdependencies and opportunities for improvement. Cross-functional teams can collaborate to brainstorm and analyze diverse perspectives, pinpointing areas that necessitate transformation and crafting comprehensive solutions for the identified challenges.

2.1.6 - Benchmarking

Compare the organization's performance, practices, and processes with industry leaders or best-in-class organizations. This approach provides a benchmark for identifying gaps and areas where the organization needs to catch up or surpass competitors. Learning from successful practices and adopting relevant strategies can help drive necessary change.

2.1.7 - Innovation and Idea Generation

Empower employees to suggest new ideas, improvements, and solutions. Implement mechanisms such as suggestion boxes, innovation challenges, or dedicated innovation teams to gather and evaluate ideas. Taking such a proactive approach to identify areas for improvement also speeds up continuous learning.

2.2 - Define the Change Objectives, Scope, and Desired Outcomes

To achieve a successful change, organizations must clearly define the change initiative's objectives, scope, and desired outcomes. Setting precise boundaries for the planned changes helps avoid scope creep and ensures focused efforts. Specify which areas of the organization will be affected by the change and identify any limitations or exclusions. This provides the following advantages:

- **Prevents Overly Ambitious Goals:** Clarity ensures that the change initiative remains grounded and realistic, preventing it from becoming too ambitious and unattainable.

- **Maintains Original Intent:** Clearly defined objectives and scope help preserve the initiative's original purpose, reducing the risk of deviations.

- **Optimizes Resource Allocation:** It facilitates better allocation of resources, ensuring that they are used efficiently and effectively.

- **Enhances Risk Management:** With a clear understanding of the change initiative, organizations can identify and manage potential risks more proactively.

- **Manages Stakeholder Expectations:** This clarity aids in managing stakeholder expectations by providing a clear roadmap of what the change aims to achieve.

- **Ensures On-Track Progress:** It helps track and measure progress, ensuring the change initiative stays on course and meets its intended goals.

The following are the key aspects to remember:

2.2.1 - Strategic Alignment

Begin by integrating the change goals with the broader strategic plan. Assess how the proposed change fits the organization's vision. This alignment ensures that the change efforts contribute to the overarching objectives.

2.2.2 - Addressing Drivers for Change

Reflect on the identified drivers for change and clearly articulate how the change objectives directly address these drivers and how they will lead to desired outcomes. This connection helps stakeholders understand the rationale behind the change and creates a sense of urgency and purpose.

2.2.3 - Measurable and Realistic Objectives

Clearly define objectives that are measurable, realistic, and time-bound. This involves setting specific targets or milestones to be tracked and evaluated throughout the change process. Quantifiable objectives provide a clear direction for progress and enable organizations to assess the impact of the change initiative. Additionally, ensuring that the goals are realistic and attainable within the available resources and constraints is essential.

2.2.4 - Risk Assessment and Mitigation

Conduct a thorough risk assessment to anticipate potential obstacles, resistance, or unintended consequences that may arise during the change process. Develop strategies and mitigation plans to address these risks and minimize their impact. This approach enhances the chances of successful implementation and helps organizations navigate potential hurdles more effectively.

2.2.5 - Continuous Adjustment and Evaluation of Change Objectives

Regularly revisit and align the change objectives and scope with the evolving organizational needs and external environment. Evaluate the progress of the change initiative against the defined goals and make adjustments accordingly. Also, be open to refining the objectives and scope based on the feedback and insights gathered during the implementation process.

2.3 - Assemble a Change Management Team

Organizations can assemble a change management team with expertise and leadership to implement successful change. The team's collaboration and effective communication contribute to its ability to navigate the complexities of change and act as catalysts for positive organizational transformation. The following are the considerations for assembling such a team:

2.3.1 - Build a Diverse and Cross-functional Team

Identify individuals with a deep grasp of change management principles, methodologies, and best practices. Seek out those with a track record of effectively guiding and facilitating impactful organizational changes. It's crucial that these professionals are not only enthusiastic about the change but also hold sway in their departments or teams.

Look for strong communicators with excellent interpersonal skills who can serve as advocates, influencers, and role models. Remember they will play a key role in raising awareness, addressing concerns, and inspiring their colleagues.

Assemble a change management team composed of individuals from different departments or fields of expertise. This diverse composition guarantees the incorporation of a wide range of viewpoints and insights during the formulation and execution of change initiatives. Ensure representation from pivotal stakeholder groups to foster collaboration and secure support for the efforts.

2.3.3 - Define Roles and Responsibilities

Clearly define the roles and responsibilities of the change management team members. Assign specific tasks and areas of focus to leverage their strengths effectively. This may include responsibilities such as change planning, communication, stakeholder engagement, required training facilitation, resistance management, and monitoring progress.

2.3.4 - Provide All-around Support

Provide comprehensive training programs or workshops to enhance the change management skills of team members. This can include courses on change management methodologies, leadership skills, communication strategies, stakeholder engagement, and conflict resolution. Equipping the team with specialized knowledge and expertise will empower them to navigate the complexities confidently.

Ensure the team has the resources, tools, and support to carry out their roles effectively. This may include access to relevant information, communication channels, budgetary support, and executive sponsorship.

Create channels to enable the team to provide feedback on the change initiatives. Encourage them to share insights, lessons learned, and suggestions for improvement. Actively listen to their feedback and integrate it into the change strategies and plans.

2.4 - Conduct a Change Readiness Assessment

Assess the organization's readiness for change by identifying potential barriers, risks, and gaps hindering successful implementation. To conduct such a comprehensive assessment, organizations should undertake the following efforts and considerations:

2.4.1 - Evaluate Organizational Culture

Review the prevalent values, beliefs, norms, and behaviors within the organization and gauge their influence on the change initiative. Identify cultural aspects that could either bolster or hinder the change process. You may observe resistance to change, a reluctance to take risks or a lack of openness to innovation within certain segments. This evaluation facilitates tailoring change strategies to leverage the organization's existing cultural strengths while effectively addressing cultural barriers.

2.4.2 - Assess Capabilities and Barriers

Begin by evaluating employees' skills, knowledge, and competencies to determine if they possess the capabilities to accept and implement the proposed change. Identify potential capacity constraints, such as financial limitations, human resource availability, time constraints, or technological limitations, which could hinder a successful change implementation. This assessment provides valuable insights into gaps that can be addressed through targeted training, optimized resource allocation, or other strategic interventions.

Furthermore, it's essential to examine factors like stakeholder resistance, conflicting priorities among leadership or different departments, incongruent policies or procedures, and communication breakdowns. Engage with stakeholders to grasp their concerns, apprehensions, and potential sources of resistance.

2.5 - Prepare for the Implementation

After taking inputs from the above evaluations, organizations must adequately prepare themselves for the upcoming transformation. Following are some practices to consider:

2.5.1 - Plan Activities and Timelines

Identify and outline specific activities required to achieve the well-defined change objectives. Break down the change initiative into manageable tasks, assigning responsibilities to individuals or teams. Establish realistic timelines for each activity, considering dependencies and resource availability. Sequencing activities strategically ensures a smooth and efficient change process, minimizing disruptions and facilitating progress.

2.5.2 - Allocate Resources and Provide Infrastructure

After the determination of the resources (financial, human, and technological) needed for the change initiative, it is essential to ensure their prompt allocation, ensuring they are accessible when required. Consider any additional resources necessary for training, communication, or stakeholder engagement.

Ensure employees can access the tools, technology, and infrastructure to support the new working methods. This may include updating software systems, equipment, or physical workspace modifications. By offering the right resources, organizations enable employees to adapt to the change and perform their roles effectively in the transformed environment.

2.5.3 - Communication Strategy

Develop a holistic communication strategy to keep stakeholders informed and engaged throughout the change. Identify key messages that need to be communicated and tailor them to different stakeholder groups. Define the appropriate communication channels, ranging from town hall gatherings and email updates to intranet portals and webinars. Reflect on the frequency and timing of communications to guarantee timely delivery of pertinent information. Effective communication serves to deepen comprehension, garner support, and adeptly address any concerns or resistance that may arise.

2.5.4 - Training and Development

Incorporate training and development strategies into the change management plan to equip employees with the required knowledge and skills to adapt to the change. Identify specific training needs based on the change impact assessment and align training programs accordingly. Provide a variety of training formats, such as workshops, e-learning modules, or on-the-job training, to cater to different learning styles.

2.5.5 - Institute Robust Support Mechanisms

Implement dedicated support mechanisms, including mentors or change champions, to provide unwavering guidance and aid for employees from the outset. Mentors serve as valuable allies, offering support, direction, and motivation to individuals grappling with challenges. Their guidance assists employees in traversing the transitional phase with confidence. Simultaneously, change champions can ardently endorse and champion the change initiative. By raising awareness, addressing concerns, and igniting enthusiasm, they rally others to embrace the transformation, thus cultivating a constructive and nurturing atmosphere.

2.5.6 - Address Resistance

Actively listen to stakeholders' perspectives and provide opportunities for them to express their thoughts and emotions. Acknowledge resistance as a natural response to change and address it empathetically. Provide transparent explanations about the change, its rationale, and anticipated benefits. Involve senior leadership and change agents who can influence and inspire their coworkers. By addressing resistance effectively, organizations can mitigate its impact and foster a more positive and supportive environment.

2.5.7 – Motivate

While providing with trainings and support systems can all help in motivating employees, we should not give lesser importance to rewards, recognition or financial incentives. Strategic and targeted financial incentives stand out as potent tools for executives to inspire and motivate employees. In a study conducted by McKinsey [4.1], companies that integrated financial incentives directly tied to transformation outcomes experienced an impressive almost fivefold increase in total shareholder returns (TSR) compared to those without such programs.

Despite the evident advantages, the same research revealed that only two-thirds of companies opt for financial incentive programs when undertaking a transformation. Resistance to adoption stems from concerns about the overall cost, apprehensions regarding potential burdens on internal support functions, and a lack of recognition for the substantial benefits that such programs can bring. These concerns can be overcome by critically designing a customized financial incentive plan. The considerable advantages, including broad voluntary engagement from employees and the expedited, efficient execution of change initiatives even at the grassroots level of the organization, underscore the compelling case for giving serious consideration to this option as a powerful motivational tool.

To achieve this, executives should invest time upfront to meticulously craft a financial incentives program that not only aligns with the change objectives but is also tailored to effectively address existing organizational constraints. For instance, while navigating the concern of overall costs associated with financial incentive programs, executives could adopt a phased implementation approach. Rather than launching a comprehensive program all at once, they might start with a pilot initiative targeting a specific department or project. This allows them to assess the program's effectiveness on a smaller scale, fine-tune its elements, and evaluate the associated costs more precisely.

Moreover, when combined with thoughtfully crafted nonfinancial incentives, financial rewards can ignite a surge of energy and enthusiasm across the organization. However, in designing such initiatives it's crucial to avoid incentivizing broad outcomes that can be challenging to link with individual performance. Connecting initiatives directly to transformation outcomes within participants' control ensures clarity and empowers them to identify and contribute effectively to the initiatives that drive meaningful change.

For instance, A startup decides initiates a pilot program to adopt agile development and production practices. This pilot program focuses on a specific project team or department within the company. establishes key performance indicators (KPIs) to measure the success of the agile adoption, such as faster time-to-market, increased product quality, and improved team collaboration. The financial incentives program is designed to directly tie rewards to the achievement of KPIs. For example, if a project team successfully delivers a product ahead of schedule with high quality, team members receive performance bonuses.

In addition to monetary rewards, the startup introduces a recognition program to acknowledge the efforts of individual team members and the team as a whole. This could include shout-outs in team meetings or acknowledgment in company communications. They also implement a continuous feedback mechanism where team members and managers regularly discuss progress, challenges, and opportunities for improvement. This ensures that the financial incentives program remains aligned with the evolving needs of the organization.

To encourage continuous learning and skill development in agile methodologies, the startup offers incentives for employees who complete relevant training programs or certifications. This not only supports the company's agile transformation but also invests in the professional growth of the team. As the agile adoption progresses, the company collects feedback from participants and monitors its overall impact on the organization. The financial incentives program is iteratively adjusted to address any emerging challenges or to further enhance success factors.

2.6 - Monitor, Evaluate, and Sustain:

After implementing a change initiative, organizations must continuously assess its progress, evaluate its effectiveness, and sustain the momentum to ensure long-term success. Following are some approaches:

2.6.1 - Regular Monitoring and Evaluation

Consistently monitor the execution of specified activities and closely track timelines, comparing them against the planned objectives. Establish agile feedback loops to gather ongoing feedback from employees and stakeholders at various levels to assess their satisfaction with the change process and identify emerging issues. Identify any deviations or challenges that may arise and take measures to address them.

It can be done through regular retrospectives, feedback sessions, or structured feedback channels. These feedback loops allow for continuous improvement, course correction, and adaptation based on real-time insights. Through constant learning and feedback, organizations can effectively monitor the progress and ensure that it remains aligned with the needs and expectations of stakeholders.

2.6.2 - Real-time Data Analytics

Implement state-of-the-art real-time data analytics tools and systems to collect and analyze pertinent data at each stage of the process. This enables organizations to track their metrics and quickly respond to emerging issues. Real-time data allows for proactive decision-making and timely interventions to ensure the change initiative stays on track. It also provides valuable insights for evaluating the impact and outcomes of the change.

2.6.3 - Continuous Communication and Reinforcement

Regularly communicate the progress, achievements, and impact of the change. Reinforce the significance of the change by sharing success stories, lessons learned, and positive outcomes. Create an environment that not only welcomes change but actively champions it by emphasizing the advantages, acknowledging actions that align with the change, and seamlessly incorporating it into everyday routines and traditions. This ensures the change becomes ingrained in the organization's DNA.

Acknowledge and celebrate small wins along the change journey. Reward individual and team efforts and milestones attained. Celebrating small successes boosts morale, fosters a sense of accomplishment, and reinforces the belief in the change.

2.6.4 - Integrate Change into Policies and Processes

Review and change existing policies, procedures, and systems to align with the change. Ensure that workflows, performance management systems, and reward structures support and reinforce the desired behaviors and outcomes of the change. Regularly assess and update these processes to adapt to evolving needs and maintain alignment with the change initiative.

Conclusion

By embracing the foundational principles of change management and prioritizing its key components like adept leadership, effective communication, innovation, agility and continuous learning, organizations can instill a culture that not only embraces change but harnesses its power to drive sustained success. It is crucial for HPOs to continually explore and refine their change management practices, thus fortifying their capacity for adaptability and resilience. Through this dedicated commitment, HPOs can wholeheartedly embrace change as the very force that propels them toward perpetual growth and enduring success.

◆◆◆

Case Study

Netflix's Evolution: From DVD Rentals to Global Streaming Giant

Netflix has undoubtedly undergone significant changes since its inception in 1997. Initially established as a movie rental service by Marc Randolph and Reed Hastings, the company swiftly recognized the transitory nature of DVDs, prompting them to conceive a more expansive aspiration: to pioneer the realm of internet-based streaming for movies and TV shows, ultimately shaping the trajectory of their vision. Three significant changes marked crucial turning points in this journey. The first was in 1999 when the company introduced the subscription option for DVD rentals, revolutionizing the rental industry by offering unlimited DVD rentals without late fees. This move redefined their business model and set the groundwork for future innovations.

The second pivotal moment occurred in 2007, when Netflix launched its online video streaming service, shaking up the entertainment landscape by transforming how movies and TV shows were consumed. This disruptive change established Netflix as a frontrunner in the streaming industry and solidified its position as a significant player in the global market. Subsequently, Netflix continued to push boundaries and challenge traditional norms.

As Netflix continued to evolve, it recognized the need to provide a diverse range of content to meet the ever-changing demands of consumers. Thus, another pivotal moment occurred when the company transformed from solely a distribution platform to a production company. In 2012, the company began producing original content, starting with the "Lilyhammer" series, followed by many original films, documentaries, specials, and miniseries. By producing its own content, Netflix expanded its library and asserted itself as a serious contender in the entertainment production arena.

This strategic shift allowed them to offer a large portion of the content available and cater to a broader audience. Netflix's ability to recognize the changing market landscape and adapt accordingly showcases its remarkable agility and foresight, positioning it as a prime example of a company that seizes emerging opportunities.

The success of Netflix's transformations can be attributed to its unique company culture and effective change management strategies. Instead of sticking to conventional parameters, Netflix positions itself as an inherently creative firm, allowing it to embrace and lead change easily. Netflix's change management process is a model for other organizations to follow. Let's see how it does it:

Embracing Diversity and Empowering Talent

Netflix has a unique culture focused on encouraging decision-making by employees, sharing information openly, communicating candidly, and keeping only highly effective people. They prioritize "people over process" and believe in fostering a dream team of talented individuals who work collaboratively. Here is what NETFLIX expects from its employees and facilitates them to accomplish:

- To make wise decisions despite ambiguity
- Use data to inform their intuition and choices
- Listen well and seek to understand before responding
- Be calm in stressful situations
- Learn rapidly and eagerly
- Take informed risks and be open to possible failure
- Seek what is best for Netflix, not themselves or their team
- Demonstrate consistently strong performance so colleagues can rely upon them
- Work well with people of different backgrounds, identities, values, and cultures
- Exhibit and be known for candor and transparency

The company operates based on the principles of freedom and responsibility. It encourages independent decision-making by employees. The company believes that giving employees more autonomy and trust will make them more innovative, efficient, and dedicated to the company's goals. Managers here act more as coaches, setting context and offering feedback rather than micromanaging.

Reed Hastings stated in an interview, "The best managers figure out how to get great outcomes by setting the appropriate context rather than by trying to control their people."

Netflix maintains a strong feedback culture, with constructive feedback being an everyday part of work life. They believe in giving and receiving feedback regularly to improve as a team. Netflix has a culture where they also communicate candidly and directly with the employees, avoiding sugarcoating or hiding unpleasant truths. They also believe that sharing information widely within the company allows employees to make better decisions and collaborate more effectively.

A central objective for Netflix is to create an inclusive and welcoming environment, ensuring every employee experiences a genuine sense of belonging. Netflix firmly believes that a critical aspect of achieving better representation on-screen is cultivating diversity and inclusion within its own workplace. The company significantly emphasizes internal efforts, recognizing their direct impact on external endeavors. It values employees from diverse backgrounds, appreciating the importance of varied perspectives and experiences in creating captivating content. This dedication is crucial in empowering employees at all levels to offer their best ideas and talents.

According to their 2022 Inclusion Report [4.2], Women comprise 49.6% of their workforce and have the highest representation at Netflix. Women leadership (Directors and above) is at 51.4%. Over half of their U.S. workforce (52.9%) comprises people from one or more historically excluded ethnic and racial backgrounds, including Asian, Black, Hispanic or Latino/a/x, Middle Eastern or North African, Native American, and Pacific Islander. Netflix has built and deepened its inclusion work by adding staff worldwide — including leaders in India, Japan, Singapore, Mexico, and Brazil.

To foster an inclusive atmosphere, Netflix relies on its Employee Resource Groups (ERGs). They have 18 ERGs serving Latino/a/x, veteran, Black, disability communities etc. These groups serve as crucial communities where employees with shared experiences can connect and find support. Netflix recognizes and supports its employees, regardless of religion, family responsibilities, gender identities, or disabilities. The company consistently analyzes and addresses pay disparities to ensure equitable employee compensation.

Netflix's commitment to inclusivity extends to its comprehensive benefits package. With offerings like a flexible parental leave policy and non-prescribed time-off policies, a family forming benefit, health benefits, as well as comprehensive care for transgender and non-binary individuals in their U.S. health plans, Netflix endeavors to cater to the diverse needs of its workforce. This approach not only strengthens their workplace culture but also reinforces their commitment to producing meaningful and resonant content that connects with audiences from all walks of life.

As companies expand, they face the risk of adopting a rigid and formal approach, resulting in challenges like excessive micromanagement, multiple cross-departmental meetings for tactic approvals, and a focus on pleasing internal groups over customer needs. This rigidity can impede efficiency and flexibility. To address these challenges, Netflix upholds the "Highly Aligned, Loosely Coupled" philosophy, a fundamental aspect of its decision-making culture, allowing teams to work independently while sharing strategic context.

Such an approach requires substantial investments in transparency, articulation, and perception of overarching goals, strategies, and context. Despite this, Netflix seeks to minimize cross-functional meetings, utilizing them primarily to align with goals and strategy rather than detailed tactics or approaches to solutions. To ensure everyone shares the same understanding, there are thorough debates and documentation. Once the strategy gains consensus, the company trusts its teams to execute tactics independently without seeking prior approval.

Candid discussions are encouraged later to address issues experienced and pave the way for future improvements. The success of this approach depends on talented individuals collaborating effectively and establishing a context that supports their collective efforts.

Leveraging Data and Data-Driven Decision Making

Data plays a crucial role at Netflix, shaping how the platform operates and interacts with its 247 million [4.3] paid subscribers worldwide (as of the second quarter of 2023). It serves as the bedrock for guiding creative decisions, providing personalized recommendations, and ensuring a seamless user experience. Through advanced data analytics, Netflix gains insights into customer behavior and preferences, allowing them to predict the success of original content, tailor marketing materials, and optimize production planning.

One unique aspect of Netflix's approach to data is the integration of data scientists into various critical business units, including product development, content creation, membership, studio marketing, and platform development. The Netflix data team is a formidable force comprising analysts, and engineers. Their mission revolves around helping Netflix understand not only its own business but also the broader global landscape.

They use advanced data analytics to deliver personalized recommendations to users, predict the popularity of original content, optimize marketing strategies, enhance production planning, and facilitate informed technical and business decision-making. Embracing a "Context not Control" culture, these data scientists are given considerable autonomy. They are free to select and prioritize projects that will significantly affect the business.

With over 80% of content streamed on Netflix [4.4] attributed to its recommendation system, data science is central to shaping the user experience. Thus, by leveraging data in this comprehensive and strategic manner, Netflix stays attuned to customer preferences and market trends, cementing its position as a leading provider of top-notch streaming entertainment.

HR Innovation

Netflix's approach to HR sets it apart from traditional methods, reflecting a unique and innovative perspective on talent management. The company's primary focus is hiring top-notch "A" players, avoiding recruiting average or below-average performers. This strategy stems from the belief that having high-performing individuals on the team fosters employee motivation and productivity.

A striking characteristic of its HR approach is the emphasis on thinking like businesspeople and innovators before thinking like traditional HR professionals. Talent managers at Netflix prioritize driving tangible business outcomes and fostering innovation, moving beyond conventional HR practices. This forward-thinking perspective ensures that HR initiatives contribute directly to the company's success and growth.

Netflix's unique approach to employee management reflects a profound trust in its workforce, treating them as mature adults capable of acting in the company's best interests. This trust is evident in various aspects of the company's policies, including its infamous vacation policy. Netflix allows its employees to take as much time off as they need as long as they continue to meet their performance expectations. By offering this level of flexibility, the company shows its confidence in employees' ability to manage their time responsibly.

Moreover, Netflix stands apart from traditional corporate structures by not imposing formal travel and expense policies or even performance reviews. Instead, the company relies on its employees' judgment and common sense to make decisions that impact the organization. This autonomy empowers employees to be self-reliant and much more confident.

Netflix also offers attractive severance packages to employees who are no longer fit for the company or their role. Instead of putting them through emotionally draining performance improvement plans (PIPs), Netflix prefers to part ways with them amicably and respectfully. This way, the company saves time and energy and avoids spoiling relationships with former employees.

In summary, Netflix's HR strategy revolves around hiring exceptional talent, providing transparent performance feedback, boosting excellence and innovation, treating employees like mature adults, and parting ways with employees respectfully when necessary. By prioritizing these fundamental principles, Netflix has built a workforce that consistently drives its success and keeps it at the forefront of the entertainment industry.

◆◆◆

Chapter 5 - Harnessing Speed and Agility for Business Excellence

In the race for business excellence, speed and agility set the pace.

Speed and agility are distinct yet interconnected concepts pivotal in building high-performance organizations. Speed refers to reducing time-to-market, accelerating decision-making processes, and executing operations efficiently, whereas agility is the capacity to adapt and respond effectively to changes in the business environment.

In the current hypercompetitive landscape, the need for speed is more critical than ever. Customers today expect rapid responses, shortened product cycles, and seamless experiences. By embracing speed, organizations can streamline operations, optimize processes, and deliver products and services faster. Ultimately, speed enables businesses to seize opportunities and outpace rivals in a world where time is of the essence.

However, speed alone is not enough to ensure success; agility must complement it. Agile organizations are known for their capacity to manage unforeseen disruptions, promptly adapt their strategies, redistribute resources, and alter their operations in response to changing circumstances. As such, at its core, agility signifies being resilient, flexible and responsive to market dynamics.

Thus, the significance of embracing speed and agility is unmistakably clear, as it empowers organizations to not only survive but thrive. However, it is equally crucial to acknowledge that organizations often encounter formidable challenges that impede their progress, particularly from within the organization. These internal obstacles can hinder advancement at every step, demanding a proactive and collaborative approach to address them. In the following section, we will delve into these obstacles and explore effective strategies to overcome them.

1 - Barriers to Speed and Agility

It is critical to identify areas where decision-making processes may slow down progress, assess the state of your technology infrastructure, and evaluate the prevailing culture and attitudes toward risk and innovation. Let us examine the following factors that impede speed and agility:

1.1 - Lack of Strategic Alignment and Collaboration

It happens especially when different departments or teams have conflicting priorities or goals. Collaboration becomes arduous when departments operate in isolation and fail to communicate effectively. These departments may pursue their own objectives without considering the broader organizational goals, which results in fragmented efforts and inefficient use of resources.

Additionally, this hampers the organization's capacity to effectively share information, exchange ideas or implement best practices. This lack of knowledge makes organizations miss out on their employees' collective expertise and experiences. The absence of effective communication channels and collaboration platforms further exacerbates this issue, impeding both individual and team advancement. This, in turn, leads to sluggish decision-making and a lack of synchronization in organizational undertakings.

1.2 - Hierarchical Decision-Making

The presence of a decision-making structure, where decision authority is primarily concentrated at the top, can significantly impede the speed and agility of an organization. In such arrangements, the decision-making process is often slowed down as approvals and consultations need to traverse up and down the hierarchy. Additionally, the complex reporting lines, multiple layers of approvals, and excessive bureaucracy inherent in these structures create bottlenecks, impeding the flow of critical information across departments and teams.

1.3 - Lack of Continuous Learning

The absence of a learning-oriented culture within an organization represents a static environment where the growth of employees takes a backseat. Without continuous learning, employees' skills become outdated, limiting the organization's potential to embrace new technologies and meet industry demands. When there is limited knowledge sharing, collaboration becomes more complex, people are less willing to accept changes, and the organization cannot maximize its internal resources.

1.4 - Resistance to Technology Adoption

This challenge looms large for organizations due to their reliance on outdated technology, legacy systems, manual processes, and a reluctance to embrace digital transformation. This hinders the adoption of beneficial technologies, obstructs automation efforts, and thwarts the organization's ability to meet the demands of the digital era. Consequently, it leads to operational inefficiencies and missed opportunities for digital transformation benefits.

1.5 - Organizational Inertia

It stems from resistance that surfaces within an organization when there is a pressing demand to adapt quickly or substantially alter operational practices, policies, or culture. Employees may exhibit reluctance because of various factors, such as:

- Fear of the unknown.

- Lack of understanding about the purpose or benefits of the change.

- Preference for the familiar status quo.

- An unconducive organizational culture where innovation and risk-taking are not encouraged.

1.6 - Insufficient resources

Having adequate resources facilitates the seamless implementation of groundbreaking processes, technologies, and initiatives. These embody the very essence of efficiency, speed, and adaptability. Time constraints can lead to rushed decision-making and inadequate planning and preparation, all of which undermine the organization's capacity to adapt quickly.

Without adequate funds, organizations may struggle to gain the tools, technologies, and resources to drive innovation and streamline operations. Insufficient financial backing can restrict the organization's capacity to invest in research, training programs, and infrastructure upgrades, thereby impeding the swift adoption of new methodologies.

Lack of expertise or a shortage of competent staff members can significantly slow the adoption of new processes and technologies and even reduce the efficiency of day-to-day operations. Without individuals who possess the skills and knowledge, organizations may encounter obstacles such as difficulty in troubleshooting problems and suboptimal utilization of tools or technologies and new systems, all of which contribute to decreased speed and agility.

2 - Strategies for Prioritizing Speed and Agility

2.1 - Adopt Agile Development

This approach can significantly enhance speed and responsiveness in project delivery. It entails adopting an iterative framework that prioritizes swiftness, collaboration, and continuous improvement. By breaking projects down into smaller, manageable tasks and working in short sprints, organizations can promote close collaboration among cross-functional teams. The iterative nature of agile empowers faster feedback cycles, facilitating prompt adjustments and enhancements.

2.2 - Embrace Lean Six Sigma

This approach combines lean manufacturing principles, emphasizing waste reduction, with Six Sigma's statistical analysis and problem-solving techniques. Through the optimization of processes, including the removal of non-value-added activities, reduction of errors, and enhancement of overall productivity, organizations can achieve significant improvements.

2.3 - Establish DevOps

This approach involves merging software development and IT operations to facilitate the swift delivery of applications and services. It necessitates fostering close collaboration among development, operations, and quality assurance teams throughout the software development lifecycle. Organizations can reduce time-to-market and enable rapid iteration by automating processes such as testing, deployment, and infrastructure management. Furthermore, implementing continuous integration and delivery (CI/CD) practices ensures a seamless and efficient software delivery pipeline.

2.4 - Be Customer-Centric

Organizations must adopt a customer-centric approach. Thorough market research and active collection of customer feedback provide valuable insights, facilitating informed decision-making. This way, they can swiftly develop products and services that resonate with the market landscape by gaining a profound understanding of customer needs and preferences.

Analyzing this customer behavior data, including purchasing patterns, website analytics, and social media engagement, allows organizations to identify trends and patterns efficiently. With this knowledge, organizations can iterate quickly, incorporating customer preferences and addressing pain points to enhance customer satisfaction and drive continuous product innovation.

2.5 - Implement a Flat Organizational Structure

As discussed in the barrier sections, an organizational structure that reduces hierarchy and bureaucracy facilitates faster decision-making, better collaboration and autonomy. So here are different ways to undergo this complicated transformation:

2.5.1 - Assess the Current Hierarchy

Conduct a comprehensive evaluation of the existing hierarchy. This involves scrutinizing the layers of management to identify redundancies and unnecessary positions. Analyze the roles and responsibilities of each management position. Determine if specific roles can be combined or if some positions can be eliminated without affecting the organization's overall effectiveness.

2.5.2 - Consider Alternative Structures

Explore different organizational structures, such as a matrix, team-based, flat, or networked approach, that promote collaboration and reduce the need for excessive management layers. Assess the feasibility and potential benefits of implementing such structures within your organization.

2.5.3 - Redefine Reporting Lines

Adjust reporting lines to minimize the number of levels between top leadership and frontline employees. Simplify the reporting structure by empowering employees to have direct access to decision-makers and reducing the need for information to pass through multiple layers of management. This not only accelerates decision-making but also enhances communication throughout the organization.

2.5.4 - Provide Training and Support

Transitioning to a flatter hierarchy requires empowering employees to take on increased responsibilities. Offer training programs to help employees develop the skills and capabilities necessary to handle increased responsibilities and make independent decisions. Facilitating mentorship also ensures a smooth transition to the flatter hierarchy.

2.5.5 - Communicate the Changes

Transparent communication is paramount when restructuring an organization. Communicate the reasons for flattening the hierarchy, including the benefits it brings to the organization and its employees. Address employee concerns or questions and emphasize the value of collaboration and shared accountability in the new structure.

To achieve this, senior leaders should embody the principles of a flat organizational structure. This involves being approachable, receptive to feedback, and actively involved with employees across all levels. To facilitate such an environment, it's also important to implement open-door policies, leverage virtual collaboration tools, and conduct regular team meetings

2.5.6 - Provide Clarity before Autonomy

Provide clear guidelines, boundaries, and accountability frameworks to ensure that decisions are always in line with the overarching goals and values. Clearly outlining decision-making authorities, empowers employees to make decisions confidently within their areas of expertise and responsibilities. Communicate expectations and responsibilities to avoid confusion and promote efficiency.

2.5.7 - Monitor and adapt

The implementation of a flat organizational structure is an ongoing process. Continuously monitor the success of the new hierarchy, gathering feedback from employees at all levels. Evaluate its impact on productivity, communication, and decision-making. Stay open to further refining the structure based on feedback and evolving organizational needs, ensuring an adaptive and responsive design.

2.6 - Encourage Rapid Prototyping

This approach entails crafting simplified versions or prototypes of products or services for obtaining feedback and validating assumptions. To implement this, organizations can utilize rapid prototyping techniques such as wireframing, mock-ups, or Minimum Viable Products (MVPs).

This iterative method commences by soliciting feedback from customers and stakeholders in the early stages of development. Conduct user testing sessions, surveys, or focus groups to gain deeper insights. These interactions provide a valuable understanding of user preferences, pain points, and areas for improvement.

Subsequently, it involves iteratively refining the offering based on their input, thus effectively aligning it with market demands. It's crucial to facilitate continuous communication and collaboration throughout this dynamic process. This ensures seamless coordination between the development team, designers, and stakeholders.

2.7 - Prioritize Scalability Planning

It entails developing comprehensive plans that define precise strategies for rapidly scaling operations in response to market demands. Conduct thorough capacity planning exercises to ensure that infrastructure, resources, and processes can effectively accommodate increased workloads or sudden surges in demand. Evaluate existing capabilities and identify any potential bottlenecks that may impede scalability.

Implementing scalable cloud-based solutions, flexible staffing models, and adaptable supply chain management facilitates prompt and smooth scaling up or down. Furthermore, regularly reviewing and updating scalability plans in response to market dynamics and growth projections proves advantageous. Through this, organizations can swiftly respond to both opportunities and challenges while maintaining operational efficiency.

2.8 - Break Down Silos between Departments

To foster collaboration across departments and teams, organizations need to cultivate a culture that highly regards collaborative efforts in tackling intricate challenges and swiftly adapting to evolving circumstances. Firstly, aligning goals and objectives across departments creates a shared purpose. Similarly, empowering individuals to reach out and collaborate with colleagues from different areas of the organization can help them improve and develop.

Establish platforms or mechanisms, such as cross-functional meetings, collaborative software platforms, or knowledge-sharing sessions. This the flow of information across organizational boundaries.

Have shared workspaces or common areas where employees from different departments can interact and collaborate spontaneously. These physical arrangements promote informal conversations and build relationships between teams. Remember, a collaborative culture unlocks the full potential of your entire workforce through a powerful synergy.

2.9 - Agile Leadership

Agile leadership is a leadership style that prioritizes adaptability, customer-centricity, collaboration, transparency, and continuous improvement. It empowers individuals and teams to self-organize, make decisions, and deliver value incrementally while fostering a culture of learning and innovation. Agile leaders serve as mentors and facilitators, supporting their teams succeed in a dynamic and ever-changing environment.

Imagine a software development team working on a project using Agile methodologies, such as Scrum. In this case, the Agile leader could be a Scrum Master or a team leader who embodies Agile principles and practices. Here's how Agile leadership might manifest in this scenario:

1. **Empowerment:** The Agile leader empowers the development team by allowing them to self-manage. Team members have the autonomy to decide how to accomplish their tasks, set their own priorities, and make technical decisions.

2. **Iterative and Incremental Progress:** The Agile leader encourages the team to work in short, time-boxed iterations, often referred to as sprints in Scrum. The team aims to deliver a potentially shippable product increment at the end of each sprint, even if it's not a complete feature.

3. **Customer-Centricity:** The Agile leader ensures the team maintains a close relationship with the product owner or stakeholders. They regularly gather feedback and make adjustments to the product based on changing requirements and customer input.

4. **Transparency:** The Agile leader promotes transparency within the team. They facilitate daily stand-up meetings where team members share progress, challenges, and impediments. The leader also helps remove obstacles that hinder the team's progress.

5. **Continuous Learning:** The Agile leader encourages a culture of continuous improvement. After each sprint, the team holds a retrospective to reflect on what went well and what could be improved. The leader helps the team implement changes and experiments with new approaches in the next sprint.

6. **Collaboration:** The Agile leader fosters collaboration by bringing together cross-functional teams (developers, testers, designers, etc.) to work on the project. They also facilitate regular ceremonies, such as sprint planning and review meetings, to ensure everyone is aligned on goals and progress.

7. **Servant Leadership:** The Agile leader mentors and coaches the team rather than a traditional "command and control" management approach. They help team members grow in their roles, remove roadblocks, and provide support when needed.

8. **Measurable Outcomes:** The Agile leader uses key performance indicators (KPIs), such as velocity, burndown charts, and customer satisfaction metrics, to measure the team's progress and identify areas for improvement.

Conclusion

The dynamic landscape of today's business world demands swift adaptation and nimble decision-making, which can only be facilitated by cultivating a culture of speed and fostering agile methodologies. The overall approach encompasses a harmonious convergence across multiple facets—ranging from the human element and organizational structure to processes, technology, and the very essence of culture itself—thus enabling the realization of the transformative potency inherently embedded within these two pivotal attributes.

◆◆◆

Case Study

The Spotify Model: Pioneering Agile Scaling for Ongoing Growth and Adaptation

Spotify is a company that has experienced significant growth, and it has successfully implemented and scaled agile practices by adopting a unique approach now known as the Spotify model. This model has played a vital role in increasing organizational innovation and productivity by prioritizing autonomy, communication, accountability, and quality.

Initially, as a startup, Spotify extensively utilized the scrum methodology to manage its innovative projects. However, as the company expanded and welcomed more employees, it faced the challenge of accommodating this growth while maintaining its agile culture. To address this, Spotify developed the Spotify model, which strongly emphasizes team autonomy and empowers individuals to achieve objectives and complete goals.

The Spotify model grants teams the freedom to organize their work in a manner that makes the most sense for them, and it is structured around four key components: Squads, Tribes, Chapters, and Guilds.

- **Squads** are cross-functional and autonomous teams, typically comprising 6-12 individuals focusing on specific feature areas. Each Squad has a unique mission guiding their work and is supported by an agile coach and a product owner. Importantly, Squads have the autonomy to determine which agile methodology or framework they will use, providing them with high flexibility in approaching their work.

- **Tribes** are formed when multiple Squads collaborate within the same feature area. Tribes play a crucial role in building alignment across Squads and typically consist of 40-150 people, ensuring effective communication and collaboration among teams working on related feature areas.

- **Chapters**, however, resemble traditional line organizations, grouping individuals with similar skills and roles together. They handle personal growth and development within their respective areas of expertise, providing individuals with support and guidance for their professional advancement.

- **Guilds**, as informal communities of interest, allow individuals from different teams to come together, share ideas, and collaborate on common challenges. They focus on knowledge-sharing and problem-solving across the organization.

The Spotify model also incorporates the concepts of Trio and Alliance. A Trio comprises a tribe lead, design lead, and product lead, ensuring that the three essential perspectives are well represented and considered when working on new functionality. In cases where multiple tribes need to collaborate on a common goal, three or more tribe trios form an Alliance, facilitating better cooperation between the tribes.

Besides these core principles, the Spotify model includes various practices designed to support collaboration and continuous delivery. These practices involve agile tools and techniques, such as daily stand-ups, sprint planning, and retrospectives, which help teams stay aligned and focused on delivering value to customers.

Leadership here is critical in supporting team autonomy and alignment within the Spotify model. Every Squad is assigned a product owner responsible for setting priorities and creating high-level roadmaps. Additionally, an agile coach is also assigned to the Squad to help improve their work through retrospectives and one-on-one meetings.

The success of the Spotify model stems from various advantages, notably its preference for less formal and rigid processes. This emphasis allows greater leeway for Squads within the organization, enabling them to maintain their work styles. Rather than mandating changes in their methods, the model concentrates on fostering alignment among Squads and propelling them toward individual team goals. This strategy minimizes hierarchical management and grants teams the freedom to select frameworks and practices that suit them best.

One more noteworthy advantage of the Spotify model is its emphasis on trust rather than stringent control. Instead of exerting strict control over employees, Spotify trusts and supports them, fostering an environment that encourages freedom to innovate. Effective managers strive to strike a delicate balance between empowering their teams with self-management and providing guidance. They skillfully cultivate a clear vision while allowing their teams to explore innovative pathways toward success.

Additionally, Spotify has implemented an architecture that enables independent releases, facilitating frequent releases to production and minimizing dependencies. This approach enhances velocity and allows squads to deliver software quickly and with minimal friction. Each Squad is encouraged to continuously improve and create models for improving their own work. The company also strongly emphasizes an improvement culture by providing dedicated resources to help teams enhance their working methods.

The Spotify model also fosters a healthy company culture based on mutual respect and focusing on joint success rather than individual egos. Within this culture, the focus is on maximizing the value of work rather than overworking employees. Teams generate ideas, conduct experiments, and measure results, making adjustments when necessary to further maximize the value of their work.

Employee satisfaction is a priority within the Spotify model, and the company continuously works to ensure its employees are happy. Squads are encouraged to define their vision of success and track their progress over time through regular "Team Health Checks." The Spotify Health Check is a workshop where teams evaluate their work using various indicators such as code quality, delivery speed, value, fun, support from leadership, and team morale.

Spotify’s teams run these health checks regularly, using their favorite sets of questions. The health check can uncover greater systemic improvement areas for a team over a longer period of time. It includes predefined questions in the areas of tech health, team health, and product health. It is increasingly common to see this done using a survey, which can make creating the subsequent visualization easier. Thus, Spotify's adoption of this unique model has allowed the company to maintain its agile culture while scaling its operations.

Chapter 6 - Driving High-Performance through Continuous Improvement

Excellence is not a destination, but a journey of continuous improvement.

Continuous improvement, often termed as continuous process improvement (CPI) or continuous quality improvement (CQI), emerges as the cornerstone of organizational excellence. This approach embodies a systematic and disciplined methodology designed to enhance an organization's processes, products, and services. It entails thoroughly examining areas ripe for improvement, a deep dive into relevant data, implementing effective solutions, and vigilant tracking of progress.

Within the realm of organizational management, continuous improvement takes center stage, enabling organizations to reach and maintain peak performance levels consistently. It's more than just solving problems - it encourages a proactive attitude that deals with potential issues before they escalate. In this environment, employees are encouraged and empowered to contribute their ideas, explore innovative solutions, and relentlessly pursue excellence.

What's more, this practice has a direct and tangible impact on elevating customer satisfaction by enhancing the quality of products and services. Organizations can align their offerings precisely with their expectations through active engagement with customers and the seamless integration of their feedback into the improvement process. This customer-centric approach bolsters customer loyalty and relationships, fueling organic business growth.

Furthermore, continuous improvement plays a pivotal role in cost reduction and bolstering organizational agility. It empowers organizations to maximize operational efficiency by identifying and eliminating process inefficiencies, streamlining operations, minimizing waste, and optimizing resource utilization. The net result is substantial cost savings, improved profitability, and enhanced adaptability. These newfound cost efficiencies unlock resources that can be strategically redirected toward future growth initiatives and investments.

1- The Continuous Improvement Process

Continuous improvement is a dynamic and iterative journey requiring a long-term commitment. It is not a one-time event or a quick fix but a holistic approach that boosts constant learning, adaptation, and refinement. Let's explore the different stages of this process:

1.1 - Identifying Areas for Improvement

Organizations should take a proactive approach in identifying areas that need attention. It is important to tap into the knowledge and experience of employees. Encouraging suggestions and ideas from frontline staff can uncover potential issues and the need for improvement in any organization segment.

Conducting process analysis is another valuable method. This involves examining existing workflows and operational procedures to pinpoint areas of inefficiency that may result in increased costs or reduced productivity. By identifying these pain points, organizations can focus on improvement efforts where they will have the most significant impact.

Furthermore, benchmarking against industry best practices establishes a reference point for comparing performance. By studying leading organizations in the industry, companies can gain insights into innovative approaches, emerging trends, and areas where they may need to catch up to their peers. Gathering customer feedback is also an effective method that provides insight into their needs and expectations.

1.2 - Analyzing Data

This analytical phase enables organizations to delve deep into the data, determine the root causes of the problems, evaluate their impact on the business, and assess potential remedies. Organizations can employ tailored data analysis techniques, such as Root Cause Analysis and Process Mapping, to meet their specific needs. The insights gained from this analysis form the foundation for designing effective improvement strategies. We will delve deeper into these methods later in the chapter.

1.3 - Developing and Implementing Solutions

This phase may involve process improvements, changes to products or services, or adopting new technologies and tools to enhance overall performance. For the solutions to be effective, feasible, and sustainable in the long run, involving all stakeholders in the development process is important. Actively engaging stakeholders and seeking their input not only ensures the consideration of diverse perspectives but also builds greater support and commitment to the proposed changes.

During this stage, organizations should focus on creating actionable plans that address the root causes of the identified issues. This includes outlining specific steps, allocating resources, and establishing clear timelines for implementation. When seeking solutions, it is always advisable to maintain a broad perspective, considering the interests of the company while remaining vigilant towards potential challenges or risks that may emerge.

Once the solutions have been developed, the organization can proceed to the implementation phase. This involves executing the plans, monitoring progress, and making necessary adjustments along the way. Regular communication, training, and support are crucial during the implementation stage to ensure smooth adoption and facilitate a seamless transition.

1.4 - Monitoring and Making Necessary Adjustments

Organizations should establish a structured schedule for regularly reviewing key performance indicators (KPIs) that are both relevant and measurable. These KPIs need to align seamlessly with the organization's objectives. This consistent tracking and analysis of indicators brings out insights into the impact of implemented solutions, allowing the identification of areas for potential enhancement.

During the phase of evaluation, it's imperative to objectively approach data collection and analysis. This involves a diligent comparison of actual results against predetermined benchmarks. Should the evaluation uncover any discrepancy between actual results and desired outcomes, organizations should take a thoughtful step back to revisit the solutions implemented. This entails a comprehensive reassessment of root causes and the exploration of alternative approaches.

2 - Key Aspects of Implementation

To effectively implement a multifaceted process like continuous improvement, it is essential to adopt a strategic approach while ensuring active employee engagement. Let's delve into some of these essential aspects:

2.1 - Foster a Conducive Culture

To cultivate an environment of perpetual learning within your organization, it is crucial to empower employees and facilitate their development. Here are some strategies to achieve this:

2.1.1 - Empowerment and Support:

Encourage employees to contribute their unique perspectives and give them the autonomy to make decisions within their expertise. Support their professional development through training programs, mentorship opportunities, and resources that help them acquire new skills and knowledge. When you create a tailored development plan that involves the employee and aligns with their career goals and aspirations, it shows your dedication to their development.

Self-directed learning is another good way to empower and support their development. Here, employees take charge of their own growth journey. Provide them access to various learning resources, such as online courses, books, and learning platforms. Encourage them to set learning goals, explore new topics, and gain skills that align with their interests and career aspirations.

2.1.2 - Psychological Safety:

Create a safe environment where employees are comfortable taking risks, sharing their ideas, and learning from failures without fear of being judged or facing adverse outcomes. In parallel, nurturing the belief that abilities can be developed through dedication and hard work further enhances psychological safety. Cultivate an atmosphere that highly regards and incentivizes curiosity, resilience, and an eagerness to learn from failures. When people believe their efforts are valued and are encouraged to take risks and share ideas, they're more likely to embrace challenges as opportunities for growth and learning.

2.1.3 - Encourage Experimentation and Collaboration

Embrace a culture that encourages employees to test new ideas and approaches, pilot projects, and even use new technologies. Provide the resources to support employees in their experimental endeavors, such as dedicated time, budget, and tools. Celebrate both successful experiments and valuable lessons learned from failures.

Foster a collaborative environment where cross-functional teams can come together to share knowledge, exchange ideas, and solve complex challenges. Encourage using digital platforms, collaborative tools, and regular team meetings to facilitate communication. By leveraging the collective intelligence of your workforce, you unlock a wealth of ideas and perspectives that drive innovation and continuous improvement.

2.1.4 - Recognition and Rewards:

Reward employees who actively engage in improvement initiatives and contribute to the organization's growth. This recognition reinforces the value of continuous learning and innovation, motivating employees to continue their efforts and inspiring others to follow suit.

2.2 Align Learning and Development with Business Goals

This alignment ensures that the learning efforts directly support the growth and overall success of the business. Here are the key steps to do this:

2.2.1 - Gain a Deep Understanding of the Organization's Strategic Objectives

To effectively align learning and development initiatives with the organization's strategic objectives, the responsible team for designing training modules should focus on developing a thorough grasp of those objectives. Regular communication with key stakeholders, including executives, department heads, and team leaders, can achieve this.

Actively participate in strategic planning sessions and thoroughly review organizational documents, such as mission statements and annual reports. To ensure a comprehensive assessment, conduct a thorough skills gap analysis by utilizing a combination of surveys, interviews, and performance evaluations. This knowledge serves well for aligning learning and development activities with the overarching business goals, ensuring that they directly contribute to the organization's strategic vision and success.

2.2.2 - Define Clear Learning Objectives

It is vital to ensure the learning objectives adhere to the SMART criteria: specific, measurable, achievable, relevant, and time-bound. Clearly articulate the desired outcomes or skills that employees should be able to demonstrate after completing the training. For instance, examples of clear learning objectives could be "Increase sales conversion rates by 10% within three months" or "Enhance customer satisfaction ratings by 15% within six months." By setting clear objectives, organizations provide a roadmap for designing targeted learning programs and enable the evaluation of their effectiveness in achieving the desired outcomes.

2.2.3 - Tailor Learning Programs

This involves considering factors such as job roles, skill levels, and individual learning preferences. To cater to different learning styles, use various instructional methods, such as e-learning modules, interactive workshops, on-the-job training, or mentorship programs. Through this tailored approach, employees can acquire the knowledge and skills in a manner that is relevant and engaging.

2.2.4 - Integrate Real World Business Scenarios

Integrate real-world business scenarios into the learning programs to provide practical context and application opportunities. This can be accomplished by incorporating case studies, simulations, or role-playing exercises that simulate authentic workplace situations. Through the use of realistic scenarios, learners can actively apply their newly gained knowledge and skills to solve problems or making informed decisions. This approach helps bridge the gap between theory and practice, enabling employees to understand the direct impact of their learning on achieving tangible business goals.

2.2.5 - Implement a Training Measurement and Evaluation system

To ensure the effectiveness of programs, it is essential to establish a robust measurement and evaluation system. This system ought to encompass metrics such as employee performance metrics, productivity improvements, or customer satisfaction ratings. Also, gathering feedback from learners and managers through various methods, including surveys, assessments, or performance reviews, provides valuable insights into the impact of the learning initiatives. Use these inputs collected to optimize the effectiveness of future learning initiatives.

2.2.6 - Engage Managers and Supervisors in Training Initiatives

To fully harness the potential of learning and development initiatives, it's essential to actively involve managers and supervisors. Arm them with the necessary tools and resources to effectively guide their teams through the learning journey. Encourage managers to regularly connect with employees, engaging in discussions about their progress, offering valuable feedback, and reinforcing the link between newly acquired skills and overarching business objectives.

By involving managers as essential participants in this process, you amplify employees' motivation. Managers have the ability to inspire team members to apply their newly acquired skills in their day-to-day tasks. This collaborative synergy between managers and employees not only enhances the effectiveness of initiatives but also guarantees congruence with organizational objectives, ultimately culminating in heightened performance.

2.3 - Leverage Technology

Organizations can harness technology to cultivate a learning-oriented and innovative culture. Consider the following ways to achieve this:

2.3.1 - Provide Accessible and User-friendly Learning Platforms

Offer a diverse range of online courses, webinars, and e-learning modules that can be accessed conveniently anytime and anywhere. Design the learning platforms with a user-centric approach, prioritizing intuitive navigation, seamless functionality, and robust search capabilities. To ensure continued relevance, regularly update the content to align with the evolving needs and advancements in the industry.

Support employees in their pursuit of continuous learning by providing convenient access to virtual libraries, online resources, and collaborative tools that facilitate seamless remote knowledge sharing. Foster flexibility and accessibility by delivering the content through mobile learning applications or platforms, enabling employees to conveniently access materials on their smartphones or tablets and engage in learning on the go.

Promote virtual collaboration by leveraging video conferencing tools, project management software, and online communication platforms to facilitate seamless connections among team members, regardless of their geographic locations. Create virtual spaces where employees can collaborate on projects, share valuable resources, and exchange innovative ideas.

2.3.2 - Implement Gamification

To enhance motivation and engagement in the learning experience, consider implementing gamification strategies. Infuse elements such as points, badges, and leaderboards to acknowledge and celebrate employees' progress and accomplishments. Create interactive challenges, quizzes, or simulations that enable learners to apply their newly gained knowledge in a fun and competitive environment.

Foster friendly competition among employees and offer incentives or prizes to ignite participation. By incorporating gamification, organizations can transform the learning process into an immersive and enjoyable journey.

2.3.3 - Offer Micro-Learning Opportunities

Enhance the effectiveness of learning initiatives by breaking down the content into bite-sized modules that can be easily consumed during short periods. Develop focused mini-courses or micro-learning modules that concentrate on specific topics or skills, making the content easily digestible and allowing employees to complete them within a few minutes.

2.4 - Encourage Collaboration and Teamwork

Collaborative learning and teamwork are crucial elements in nurturing a learning-oriented culture and driving innovation. This empowers employees to leverage their collective expertise and achieve sustainable growth and success. Here are key strategies for it:

2.4.1 - Promote Cross-Functional Opportunities

Facilitate individuals from different backgrounds and expertise to work together on projects and initiatives. Create cross-functional teams with representatives from various departments or functions to encourage diverse perspectives and interdisciplinary collaboration.

2.4.2 - Capture and Share Best Practices and Facilitate Knowledge Sharing

Establish a culture of knowledge sharing by making knowledge and information easily accessible to all employees. We will delve deeper into this in the next chapter.

2.4.3 - Encourage Communities of Practice

These communities bring together individuals with similar interests or expertise, providing a platform for knowledge exchange, and learning. Encourage employees to join or create communities of practice related to their areas of interest. These communities can meet virtually and in person regularly to share insights, discuss challenges, and explore innovative solutions.

2.5 - Tools and Techniques for Continuous Improvement

Continuous improvement relies on utilizing diverse tools and techniques to identify potentials for betterment, analyze data, and develop effective solutions. As we strive to construct high-performance organizations, let's acquaint ourselves with some of the most prevalent and impactful tools and techniques utilized in continuous improvement:

2.5.1 - Process Mapping

Process mapping is a highly effective visual tool employed to meticulously illustrate a process, offering a detailed and organized portrayal. It elevates understanding by presenting a precise and structured outline of the process's various steps, the flow of activities, and how different components interact. This visual representation empowers stakeholders to rapidly grasp the sequence of actions, the inputs and outputs, and how everything fits together.

The utility of process mapping lies in its ability to provide crystal-clear insights. It enables organizations to:

1. **Identify Bottlenecks:** By mapping out the process, organizations can pinpoint areas where work slows down or accumulates, helping them to target these bottlenecks for improvement.

2. **Uncover Inefficiencies:** Process maps reveal inefficiencies and redundancies, shedding light on aspects of the process that can be streamlined or optimized for better efficiency and resource utilization.

3. **Highlight Communication Gaps:** It's easy to spot communication breakdowns or gaps in the process when it's visualized. This insight enables organizations to improve coordination and collaboration among teams or departments.

4. **Detect Duplicate Activities:** Process mapping can unveil instances where the same task is performed redundantly within the process, leading to potential time and resource savings when rectified.

5. **Optimize Resource Allocation:** By understanding the process in detail, organizations can better allocate resources, ensuring that they are distributed where they are needed most.

6. **Standardize Procedures:** Process mapping sets the stage for standardizing procedures, ensuring that everyone follows a consistent approach, which can enhance quality and reduce errors.

7. **Support Decision-Making:** With a clear picture of the process, decision-makers can make informed choices about where to invest resources for process improvement.

In essence, process mapping is a transformative tool that turns complex processes into transparent, digestible visuals. It empowers organizations to uncover opportunities for enhancement, streamline operations, and make data-driven decisions, ultimately driving efficiency and effectiveness in their workflows.

2.5.2 - Root Cause Analysis

Root cause analysis is a systematic approach to problem-solving that focuses on uncovering the fundamental or underlying causes of an issue. It operates by asking a series of "why" questions repeatedly, probing deeper and deeper into the problem until the true root cause is exposed. This method serves as a crucial tool for organizations seeking to not just resolve immediate issues but to truly understand the origins of problems and develop precise solutions.

In a business context, root cause analysis has several use cases, including:

1. **Quality Improvement:** Businesses often use root cause analysis to identify the root causes of defects or quality issues in their products or services. By addressing these underlying causes, they can improve overall product quality and customer satisfaction.

2. **Process Improvement:** When processes aren't performing as expected or are causing bottlenecks, root cause analysis can help uncover the reasons behind these inefficiencies. Organizations can then make targeted process improvements to enhance productivity and efficiency.

3. **Risk Mitigation:** In risk management, root cause analysis can be employed to understand the root causes of accidents, incidents, or compliance breaches. This helps organizations take preventive measures to reduce the likelihood of such events recurring.

4. **Customer Complaints:** Root cause analysis can be used to investigate the underlying reasons for customer complaints or service failures. By addressing these root causes, businesses can improve customer experiences and loyalty.

5. **Employee Performance:** When there are issues with employee performance or satisfaction, root cause analysis can be used to identify the underlying factors affecting employees. This can lead to targeted HR and management interventions to address these issues.

6. **Supply Chain Optimization:** In supply chain management, organizations can use root cause analysis to identify the causes of delays, shortages, or disruptions in the supply chain. This helps in devising strategies to mitigate risks and improve overall supply chain resilience.

7. **Cost Reduction:** Root cause analysis can help organizations identify the root causes of excessive costs or resource utilization. This information can guide cost reduction efforts and lead to more efficient resource allocation.

8. **Safety Enhancement:** In safety-critical industries, such as manufacturing and healthcare, root cause analysis is crucial for investigating accidents, incidents, or near misses. It helps in understanding the underlying factors contributing to safety issues and implementing preventive measures.

In essence, root cause analysis goes beyond addressing the symptoms of problems; it delves deep into the factors that give rise to these symptoms. By understanding and mitigating root causes, organizations can create lasting solutions, improve overall performance, and prevent recurrent issues, ultimately driving efficiency and effectiveness in their operations.

2.5.3 - Six Sigma

Six Sigma, a comprehensive methodology, emerges as a powerful strategy aimed at elevating product and service quality by systematically reducing defects. This data-driven approach employs rigorous statistical analysis to uncover the underlying causes of defects and then applies precise solutions to address them. At its core, Six Sigma's primary objective is to tighten the reins on process variation, ultimately bringing it under control and minimizing the incidence of defects and errors.

This methodology follows a structured approach known as **DMAIC**, which stands for **Define, Measure, Analyze, Improve, and Control**. Each step in the DMAIC process plays a critical role in the pursuit of enhanced quality and reduced defects. Here's a brief breakdown of what each phase entails:

- **Define:** In this phase, organizations establish a clear understanding of the problem or issue at hand. They define the scope of the project, set objectives, and identify key stakeholders.

- **Measure:** In the measurement phase, organizations gather data to assess the current state of the process under scrutiny. This involves collecting relevant data points and metrics to gain insights into the process's performance.

- **Analyze:** Armed with data, the analysis phase digs deep to identify the root causes of defects. Statistical tools and techniques are leveraged to uncover underlying issues that contribute to defects.

- **Improve:** With a firm grasp of the problems and their causes, organizations move to the improvement phase. Here, they implement targeted solutions and modifications to the process to eliminate defects and enhance overall performance.

- **Control:** The final phase, control, ensures that the improvements made are sustained over time. It involves implementing controls and monitoring mechanisms to prevent the recurrence of defects.

Now, in terms of which companies can benefit from Six Sigma, it's important to note that Six Sigma isn't industry-specific. Instead, it's a methodology that can be applied across a wide range of industries, from manufacturing and healthcare to finance and service sectors. Any organization that values quality improvement, process optimization, and reducing defects can benefit from implementing Six Sigma principles and methodologies. Whether you're producing physical products or offering intangible services, if you aim to deliver consistent high-quality outcomes, Six Sigma can be a valuable tool in your arsenal.

2.5.4 - Lean Methodology

The Lean methodology is a structured framework aimed at optimizing processes through the minimization of wasteful practices and the maximization of efficiency. At its core, Lean is all about refining workflows, shortening cycle times, and elevating overall quality. The foundation of Lean thinking is the concept of value, which is defined by what the customer expects and values. Organizations following the Lean philosophy prioritize the delivery of value to their customers while simultaneously eliminating any wastage and activities that do not contribute to that value.

Furthermore, the Lean methodology places a strong emphasis on two key principles:

1. **Visual Management:** Lean organizations leverage visual management tools such as Kanban boards and visual performance metrics. These tools provide real-time insights into the status of processes, enhancing communication and teamwork among team members. Visual management makes it easier to track progress, identify bottlenecks, and respond quickly to changes or issues.

2. **Standardized Work Processes:** Standardization is another cornerstone of Lean. It involves creating and adhering to consistent, standardized work processes. This not only ensures uniformity but also reduces errors and empowers employees to carry out their tasks with greater efficiency. Standardization fosters a culture of innovation and employee engagement while enabling organizations to be more responsive in meeting customer requirements.

The usefulness of the Lean methodology extends across various industries and organizations. Here are some key benefits and applications:

- **Manufacturing:** Lean principles were initially developed in manufacturing settings and remain highly relevant. They help reduce production lead times, minimize defects, and optimize inventory management.

- **Service Industries:** Lean can be applied to service industries such as healthcare, finance, and hospitality to streamline processes, reduce waiting times, and enhance customer experiences.

- **Software Development:** In software development, Lean principles can improve project management, increase collaboration among teams, and reduce software defects.

- **Supply Chain Management:** Lean practices can optimize supply chain processes, reducing costs and improving the overall efficiency of the supply chain.

- **Healthcare:** Lean has been successfully applied in healthcare to enhance patient care, reduce wait times, and eliminate waste in hospital processes.

- **Construction:** Lean principles can help construction companies improve project scheduling, reduce waste in materials and resources, and enhance overall project efficiency.

In essence, the Lean methodology is a versatile approach that can be adapted to virtually any industry or organization. Its core principles of value creation, visual management, and standardized work processes enable organizations to drive efficiency, improve quality, and respond effectively to customer needs and market changes.

2.5.5 - Kaizen

Kaizen, a Japanese term that translates to "continuous improvement," is a method centered around making incremental enhancements to processes. It places a strong emphasis on the notion that small, ongoing improvements can accumulate to yield significant benefits over time. At its core, Kaizen holds the belief that everyone within an organization, regardless of their position, can contribute to and reap the rewards of process improvement. It encourages employees at all levels to identify areas for improvement, propose innovative ideas, and implement changes within their sphere of influence.

One of the key principles of Kaizen is the concept of **Gemba**, which essentially means "going to the place where the work is done." This involves first-hand observation of processes, data collection, and engaging with employees who are directly involved in the work. By immersing themselves in the actual work environment and involving those who execute the tasks, organizations gain invaluable insights into existing inefficiencies and bottlenecks.

Kaizen also places a significant emphasis on data and metrics as the basis for measuring performance and guiding improvement efforts. Visual management tools such as performance dashboards and process metrics play a crucial role in tracking progress and communicating improvement initiatives. This data-driven approach empowers organizations to make informed decisions based on factual information. It enables them to prioritize improvement projects according to their potential impact on overall performance, ensuring that resources are allocated to the most impactful areas.

In essence, Kaizen is a philosophy that champions the idea that continuous improvement is achievable by fostering a culture of collaboration, data-driven decision-making, and ongoing small-scale enhancements. It is useful across various industries and organizations by promoting efficiency, reducing waste, enhancing quality, and ultimately driving sustainable growth and success.

2.5.6 - Total Quality Management (TQM)

Total Quality Management (TQM) is a comprehensive approach to continuous improvement that centers on the relentless pursuit of customer satisfaction. At the core of TQM is the belief that quality should be embedded in every aspect of an organization's operations. It requires a mindset shift, where everyone in the organization takes responsibility for the quality of their work and strives for excellence in delivering products and services.

TQM prioritizes understanding customer needs and expectations. Companies that adopt this approach put effort into gathering customer feedback, conducting market research, and engaging in customer-centric activities to understand their preferences and needs. This helps them gain valuable insights and improve their products or services accordingly.

It also involves using quality tools and techniques, such as statistical process control and benchmarking, to drive improvement initiatives. Organizations implementing TQM establish performance metrics and use data-driven approaches to monitor and evaluate quality performance. This enables them to identify trends, detect deviations, and take corrective actions to prevent quality issues and ensure continuous improvement. Thus, TQM helps organizations reduce costs associated with defects, rework, and customer complaints, improving operational efficiency and financial performance.

Conclusion

The integration of continuous improvement serves as a potent catalyst for organizations dedicated to attaining higher echelons of performance excellence. This tireless pursuit is underpinned by an array of methodologies, including Process Mapping, Root Cause Analysis, Six Sigma, Lean Methodology, and Kaizen. These methodologies act as discerning lenses, enabling organizations to precisely identify inefficiencies, reduce wastage, and refine their overall performance dynamics.

An inherent facet of this philosophy is its profound emphasis on the comprehensive development of employees. Organizations adhering to this ethos acknowledge that genuine progress encompasses the growth and evolution of their workforce. This transformative journey toward embracing continuous improvement not only revitalizes operations but also weaves into the very fabric of organizational culture. By instilling a mindset grounded in perpetual advancement, organizations inherently foster adaptability and responsiveness to the dynamic demands of the market.

This cultivation transcends theoretical concepts, as organizations actively seek customer feedback, align their trajectory using key performance indicators, and leverage data-driven insights to guide their decisions. The evolutionary approach encapsulates an unwavering dedication to constant growth, enabling organizations to consistently meet and surpass customer expectations while surging ahead of competitors in an intensely competitive business landscape.

◆◆◆

Case Study

Toyota's Continuous Improvement Journey

Toyota, the world-renowned Japanese automotive manufacturer, has become a global symbol of excellence, innovation, and efficiency. Central to Toyota's enduring success is its unwavering commitment to the philosophy of continuous improvement. Since its inception, the company has strived to create a culture that embraces change, empowers employees, and drives relentless improvement in all operations.

Toyota's continuous improvement journey began post-World War II when the company faced challenging economic conditions and resource constraints. Seeking innovative ways to optimize production and deliver high-quality vehicles, Toyota's founder, Sakichi Toyoda, and his son, Kiichiro Toyoda, laid the foundation for the Toyota Production System (TPS). This revolutionary manufacturing philosophy, which later became known as lean manufacturing, emphasized eliminating waste, efficient use of resources, empowering employees to identify and solve problems, and, most importantly, commitment to continuous improvement, which is deeply ingrained in every aspect of this system.

The lessons that can be learned from Toyota's continuous improvement journey extend well beyond the automotive and manufacturing industries. While it is deeply rooted in manufacturing processes, the principles and philosophies it embodies are adaptable and valuable across a wide range of sectors. It emphasizes the importance of embracing change, fostering a culture of innovation, involving employees at all levels, and committing to relentless improvement. Let's analyze how Toyota creates a culture where problem-solving is ingrained in the company's DNA.

The Pillars of Toyota's Continuous Improvement Culture

Kaizen Philosophy: Pursuit of Incremental Improvements

At the heart of Toyota's approach to continuous improvement lies the Kaizen philosophy. Kaizen, which translates to "change for the better" emphasizes the relentless pursuit of small, incremental improvements in all aspects of the business. Toyota believes significant improvements can result from the cumulative effect of many small changes over time. Regardless of their position, every employee is encouraged to contribute ideas and suggestions for improvement. This way Toyota ensures that the company remains flexible, adaptive and ahead of the competition.

Respect for People: Empowering Employees for Better Ideas and Innovation

Toyota's management philosophy is distinguished by its deep respect for its employees. The company acknowledges that its success heavily relies on the collective efforts of its staff. They believe that the best ideas for improvement often come from those working closest to the tasks. Following 'The Toyota Way,' the core of their culture, they prioritize diverse perspectives, turning differences into a team strength. With an essential value for people, Toyota aims to cultivate an environment where everyone feels welcome, safe, and heard, enabling all to contribute their best toward meaningful goals.

The company actively empowers its employees to engage in decision-making processes. Its success is significantly credited to its distinctive culture, which fosters an environment where frontline workers are encouraged to propose and implement local improvements. This culture thrives mutual trust and respect between management and the workforce.

At Toyota, workers are motivated to suggest improvements, driven by a sense of pride in enhancing work conditions and a spirit of camaraderie. The company rewards the entire team behind an improvement rather than singling out individuals. Senior managers display respect for those distant from the executive suite by personally visiting the front lines where they actively listen and engage with workers, thereby boosting morale. Initiatives like "Quality Circles" form small, voluntary groups wherein employees collaboratively identify and solve work-related issues within their areas of expertise, ultimately enhancing product quality and operational efficiency.

Toyota establishes standard procedures as a baseline for work execution, aiming to drive improvement and ensure the implementation of organizational objectives at the ground level. When front-line workers identify issues, they have a structured method to suggest improvements. Their suggestions undergo assessment within a quality circle comprising their peers and then require approval from their manager. Upper-level managers review these ideas and take action, illustrating a bottom-up rather than top-down approach.

Also, the front-line workers possess an intimate understanding of the significance and value of each standard procedure. They hold the necessary skills, knowledge, and a comprehensive end-to-end process perspective to solve problems. Supervisors play a crucial role in nurturing these competencies by ensuring the correct implementation of standard procedures and that workers strictly adhere to them. They encourage process improvement through coaching, questioning (as opposed to giving orders), and prompting front-line workers to think and take responsibility.

Managers motivate workers by engaging them in discussions to communicate the corporate vision. Toyota places substantial emphasis on investing in training and development programs to equip employees with the essential skills required for continuous improvement. This level of empowerment significantly boosts morale and fosters a sense of ownership among employees, resulting in a more engaged and productive workforce.

Genchi Genbutsu: Emphasizing On-the-Ground Observation and Understanding

Genchi Genbutsu, a Japanese term meaning "go and see for yourself," reflects Toyota's commitment to gathering information directly from the source. Toyota believes that to truly understand a situation or identify opportunities for improvement, one must be physically present where the action is taking place. This principle encourages managers and engineers to spend time on the shop floor, observing production processes and interacting with frontline workers. By gaining firsthand knowledge and insights, Toyota effectively addresses the root causes of the issues.

Standardization and Documentation: Establishing Best Practices

In the pursuit of consistency and quality, Toyota greatly emphasizes standardization and documentation of best practices. Rather than relying on individual brilliance, the company seeks to create standardized processes that can be replicated across different departments and locations. Standardization ensures uniformity and serves as a foundation for continuous improvement. Moreover, documenting best practices helps share knowledge and facilitates the transfer of expertise to new employees.

Jidoka: Building Quality into the Production Process

Jidoka, often translated as "automation with a human touch," is an essential pillar of Toyota's production system. This principle involves building quality in the manufacturing process at every stage. If a defect is detected during production, the process automatically stops, and the issue is immediately addressed, preventing the production of defective products. Jidoka ensures that quality issues are caught early and encourages problem-solving and root-cause analysis, leading to continuous product and process design improvement.

Just-in-Time (JIT): Reducing Waste and Inventory

The Just-in-Time (JIT) principle is one of the most famous aspects of Toyota's production system. It strives to reduce waste by producing precisely what is necessary, exactly when it is needed, and in the required quantity. This approach helps in reducing inventory levels, which, in turn, lowers carrying costs and frees up valuable space on the shop floor. By implementing JIT, Toyota can respond quickly to changing customer demands, reduce lead times, and improve overall efficiency in its production process.

The Toyota Way: Guiding Principles for Continuous Improvement

Toyota has achieved unparalleled success through its renowned management philosophy "The Toyota Way." This set of guiding principles serves as the foundation for Toyota's continuous improvement culture and has propelled the company's success over the years. Let's delve into each of these principles and understand their significance in driving Toyota's continuous improvement journey:

Base Decisions on Long-Term Goals

Toyota's approach to decision-making revolves around a long-term perspective. Instead of focusing solely on short-term gains, the company prioritizes strategies and actions that align with its long-term goals and vision. This principle helps Toyota resist the temptation of quick fixes and allows it to invest in sustainable solutions that bring lasting benefits to the organization, its employees, and its customers.

Develop a Consistent System for Highlighting Issues in the Workflow

Toyota places great emphasis on establishing smooth process flows. By optimizing the flow of materials and information, problems and inefficiencies are brought to the surface more quickly. This enables the company to promptly address issues, engage in proactive problem-solving, and prevent larger disruptions down the line.

Use "Pull" Systems to Avoid Overproduction

Overproduction can lead to excessive inventory and waste. Toyota employs pull systems, where production is based on actual customer demand. This ensures that goods and services are only produced when needed, reducing excess inventory and associated costs while maintaining the flexibility to adapt to changing market demands.

Level Out the Workload

Fluctuations in production levels can strain resources and lead to inefficiencies. Toyota aims to level out the workload through careful planning and production scheduling. Maintaining a stable and consistent production pace can improve resource utilization, reduce employee stress, and enhance overall productivity.

Stopping to Fix Problems

Toyota encourages a culture where employees are empowered to stop production if they encounter any quality issues or abnormalities. This principle instills employee responsibility and ownership and ensures that problems are addressed immediately, preventing defects from being passed downstream in the production process.

Standardize Tasks

Standardization is a critical element of Toyota's continuous improvement philosophy. By establishing standardized work procedures, the company can create a baseline for performance and identify improvement areas more quickly. Moreover, standardization facilitates knowledge sharing and smooth knowledge transfer across teams and generations of employees.

Use Visual Control to Ensure No Problems Are Hidden

Visual management is a crucial aspect of Toyota's operational approach. The company uses visual tools such as Kanban boards, Andon systems, and performance dashboards to make information and potential issues readily visible to everyone in the organization. This transparency ensures problems are promptly identified and addressed.

Use Only Reliable, Thoroughly Tested Technology

Toyota emphasizes using reliable and thoroughly tested technology in its production processes. This principle ensures that the company invests in proven efficient technologies, minimizing the risk of disruptions because of technological failures.

Grow Leaders Who Thoroughly Understand the Work

To sustain continuous improvement, Toyota prioritizes developing leaders who deeply understand the work. These leaders are expected to be intimately involved in the processes they oversee, enabling them to make informed decisions, support their teams, and drive improvements based on practical knowledge and experience.

Develop Exceptional People and Teams

Toyota invests in its workforce through rigorous training programs tailored to individual roles, ensuring that employees are equipped with the needed skills and knowledge. The company empowers employees by providing autonomy in decision-making, enabling them to take ownership of their work and contribute innovative ideas. Toyota's recognition and reward systems motivate employees to keep on improving.

Respecting the Extended Network of Partners and Suppliers:

Toyota nurtures long-term partnerships with its suppliers, promoting transparency and open communication. The company collaborates closely with suppliers to ensure shared goals and align strategies, resulting in efficient supply chains and high-quality components. Toyota emphasizes mutual growth and supports suppliers' development, forging strong collaborative relationships.

Go and See for Yourself for Leadership:

Toyota's leaders practice "genchi genbutsu," (explained earlier) by going to the actual location (genchi) and observing the actual product (genbutsu) to gain firsthand understanding. This mindset enables leaders to identify inefficiencies, engage with frontline employees, and address issues promptly, leading to effective decision-making.

Make Decisions Slowly by Consensus, Act Quickly on Agreed-Upon Plans:

Toyota's decision-making process involves extensive discussions and consensus-building, considering input from various stakeholders to reach well-informed decisions. However, once decisions are made, Toyota acts swiftly to implement plans, minimizing delays and ensuring timely responses to market demands.

Become a Learning Organization:

Toyota encourages employees to continually attend workshops, seminars, and courses to enhance their skills and knowledge. The company encourages reflection and improvement by holding regular meetings to review past performance and identify areas for growth. Toyota also encourages employees to experiment with new ideas and technologies to drive continuous organizational improvement.

Tools and Techniques for Continuous Improvement at Toyota

Let's inspect some of the key tools and techniques that have played a crucial role in Toyota's quest for excellence:

PDCA (Plan-Do-Check-Act) Cycle: The Foundation for Problem-Solving

The PDCA cycle, also known as the Deming Cycle or the Shewhart Cycle, is a fundamental problem-solving approach at Toyota. It comprises four stages: Plan, Do, Check, and Act. During the Plan phase, potential issues are identified, and improvement goals are set. In the Do phase, the planned changes are implemented on a small scale. The Check phase involves evaluating the results to determine if the changes were effective. Finally, successful changes are standardized and implemented on a broader scale in the Act phase. The PDCA cycle ensures a systematic and iterative approach to problem-solving, promoting continuous learning and improvement.

5 Whys: Root Cause Analysis for Effective Problem-Solving

The 5 Whys is a simple yet powerful technique Toyota uses for root cause analysis. When a problem arises, the method involves asking "why" multiple times (usually five) to uncover the underlying cause of the issue. By delving deeper into the cause-and-effect relationships, Toyota can directly identify and address the root cause rather than just treating the symptoms. This method prevents recurring problems and fosters a deeper understanding of the processes involved.

Kanban: Visual Management and Inventory Control

Kanban is a visual management tool used by Toyota to facilitate workflow and manage inventory levels effectively. It involves using visual cards or signals to highlight the need to produce or replenish materials. Kanban allows teams to identify workflow imbalances quickly, ensure production is aligned with demand, and avoid overproduction. By visually representing work status and progress, Kanban enables better communication and coordination among team members.

Poka-Yoke (Error-Proofing): Preventing Mistakes Before They Occur

Poka-Yoke, a Japanese term meaning "mistake-proofing" or "error-proofing," is a technique Toyota employs to prevent defects or errors from occurring in the first place. This involves implementing mechanisms or safeguards in the production process that make it impossible or highly unlikely for mistakes to happen. Poka-Yoke devices may include sensors, guides, or physical design changes that prevent incorrect assembly or usage, ultimately improving product quality and reducing rework or defects.

Andon: System for Notifying Problems in Real-Time

The Andon system is a real-time visual notification tool used on Toyota's production lines. When a problem or abnormality is detected, workers can activate the Andon by pulling a cord or pressing a button. This immediately alerts team leaders and support staff, enabling them to quickly resolve the issue. The Andon system encourages workers to take ownership of quality and fosters a culture where problems are addressed promptly, leading to continuous improvement.

Heijunka (Production Smoothing): Balancing Production to Meet Demand

Heijunka, also known as production smoothing, is a technique Toyota uses to level out production schedules and meet customer demand more efficiently. Rather than producing large batches of a single product, Heijunka involves making smaller quantities of various products in a balanced manner. This approach helps Toyota respond better to fluctuations in customer demand and minimizes the impact of production disruptions, resulting in reduced inventory, lead times, and waste.

Value Stream Mapping: Identifying Waste and Inefficiencies

Value Stream Mapping is a lean management tool that Toyota uses to analyze and optimize the flow of materials and information in its processes. By mapping the entire value stream from the start to the end of a process, Toyota can identify bottlenecks, redundancies, and non-value-added activities. This analysis enables the company to eliminate waste, reduce cycle times, and optimize overall process efficiency.

Conclusion

Toyota's continuous improvement journey has not only shaped the automotive industry but has also made an enduring impact on the principles of modern management. The company's relentless pursuit of excellence, underpinned by its commitment to the Toyota Way (Continuous Improvement and Respect for People), has set a benchmark for organizations worldwide. Toyota's commitment to continuous improvement remains unwavering, and its legacy is a source of inspiration for organizations seeking to navigate the challenges of a dynamic business landscape.

◆◆◆

Chapter 7 - Leveraging Knowledge for Success

In the digital age, organizational knowledge is the new currency of competitiveness.

Efficiently managing knowledge and information is a crucial determinant of success today. Knowledge management revolves around the strategic handling of invaluable assets, such as intellectual capital and expertise, specifically emphasizing transforming tacit knowledge into explicit insights that can be readily disseminated.

Concurrently, information management encompasses collecting, organizing, and administering data to ensure its precision, accessibility, and usability. This wide-ranging scope includes structured data, documents, records, and various information categories housed within databases and systems. It also encompasses crucial functions like data governance, quality control, security, and lifecycle management, all of which play a pivotal role in safeguarding the integrity and worth of the data.

According to Deloitte's Global Human Capital Trends study in 2021 [7.1], 'knowledge management' is ranked as one of the top three factors influencing a company's success. However, only an astonishingly low 9 percent of surveyed organizations feel adequately prepared to address this pressing concern. The study emphasizes the need for a shift from knowledge capture to knowledge creation and transfer. It signifies the importance of fostering a knowledge-sharing culture.

Establishing effective knowledge and information management framework can significantly liberate employees' time for more productive tasks, fostering an environment conducive to heightened innovation and revenue generation. In the subsequent sections, we will delve into the myriad benefits of this approach and explore how organizations can harness the power of effective knowledge-sharing practices.

1 - Benefits of Knowledge Sharing System:

1.1 - Enhanced Decision-Making and Risk Mitigation

The increasing number of diverse sources of information and data in the modern workplace adds complexity to the process. Workers often spend a considerable portion of their workday searching for information, leading to concerns about productivity and time management. Effective information management ensures that relevant and accurate data and information are readily available to decision-makers. Knowledge sharing enables individuals to share their expertise, insights, and lessons learned, providing a broader knowledge base. It aids in steering clear of repeating past errors, paving the way for more informed and improved decision-making in the future.

Organizing and keeping information in one place that's easy to reach helps organizations prevent data from being isolated and ensures that decision-makers get the information they need when needed. This allows them to see trends, patterns, and useful insights. It also helps them spot new risks and challenges early, giving them the chance to come up with plans to deal with them.

1.2 - Driving Innovation and Competitive Advantage

Knowledge sharing allows employees to exchange ideas, insights, and best practices. This exchange of expertise fuels creativity and sparks innovation by enabling employees to build upon each other's ideas, identify new opportunities, and develop novel solutions. By tapping into the organization's collective intelligence, companies can generate innovative products, services, and processes that differentiate them from competitors.

Furthermore, organizations prioritizing knowledge sharing and information management are better positioned to respond to changing market conditions and customer demands. By collecting and analyzing relevant information about market trends, customer preferences, and emerging technologies, organizations can pinpoint gaps and opportunities for innovation. This knowledge enables organizations to tailor their offerings quickly in order to keep pace with evolving customer expectations. Ultimately, this enhances customer satisfaction and loyalty, further strengthening their competitive position in the market.

1.3 - Maximizing Performance and Resilience

Knowledge management speeds up the learning process. Lessons learned from past projects, best practices, and success stories can be shared, allowing employees to build on existing knowledge. It enables them to perform their tasks more effectively, avoiding redundant efforts and promoting continuous improvement. Access to knowledge enhances job satisfaction and creates a nurturing work environment.

Creating platforms and tools for knowledge sharing breaks down silos and promotes cross-functional collaboration. This ensures that organizations can swiftly adapt to changes, draw insights from past successes and failures, and apply knowledge to navigate challenges. The progressively built-up resilience empowers organizations to remain stable and responsive in the face of disruptions.

Also, by capturing and documenting knowledge, organizations ensure the retention of critical information, even when employees retire, switch roles, or move to new organizations. This preservation of institutional knowledge enables continuity and prevents the loss of valuable insights.

1.4 - Employee Engagement and Retention

In the current landscape dominated by digital-native workers, this stands out as one of the noteworthy benefits of Knowledge Management (KM). These individuals, particularly from Generation Z, have high expectations driven by their lifelong exposure to technology. They expect easy and all-time access to the information relevant to not only their roles and domains but also the organization and the industry in which they work. The inability to find urgently needed information on a weekly basis affects almost three in ten workers. This impediment not only impacts productivity but also employee satisfaction and retention.

According to a study done by Coveo [7.2], most workers (86%) are slowed or prevented from finding needed information for many reasons: multiple application storage (44%); irrelevant or outdated info in company intranet (31%); or not knowing where to look (30%). An astonishing 88% of workers experience demoralization when they are unable to locate the necessary information required for their tasks. Effective knowledge management can alleviate these issues by ensuring that employees have efficient access to the information they need, thereby enhancing job satisfaction and retention rates.

2 - Barriers to Effective Knowledge Management

Understanding the challenges an organization can face while implementing such a broad and complex internal system is crucial to maximizing its benefits. Some common barriers include:

2.1 - Resistance to Knowledge Sharing

One significant challenge is the attitude of information hoarding among employees, where individuals or departments withhold knowledge to maintain power or a competitive advantage. This resistance emerges due to concerns about losing individual expertise, relevance, and even job security within the organization. Employees may be reluctant to share their knowledge, fearing it will diminish their perceived value or jeopardize their position.

This behavior often arises from a hierarchical setup or a competitive workplace atmosphere that places greater importance on individual achievement than on teamwork or organizational success. A lack of trust and psychological safety in the workplace can also influence resistance to knowledge sharing. Employees may also hesitate if they feel their ideas will be dismissed, stolen, or not adequately recognized. This can lead to a fragmented work environment, where critical knowledge remains isolated and not effectively shared.

2.2 - Inadequate Technology Infrastructure and Processes

Lacking a strong knowledge management platform or appropriate technological tools, sharing knowledge can become quite challenging. Weak infrastructure constrains the capability to capture, store, retrieve, and share knowledge. Employees might face difficulties accessing vital information if they encounter obstacles like limited search abilities, ineffective information arrangement, or insufficient training on knowledge management tools and systems. In addition to technology, having well-established processes and frameworks is vital for effective knowledge management. Without clear guidelines and procedures, employees might find it hard to grasp how and where to access information.

2.3 - Lack of Adequate Organizational Culture

In a culture that doesn't prioritize knowledge sharing, valuable insights tend to get isolated and left unused. When an open and collaborative atmosphere is lacking, knowledge struggles to flow smoothly between different teams and departments. Building a culture of sharing requires strong leadership support. Without leaders championing knowledge management, the effectiveness of such endeavors can be compromised.

Moreover, if employees aren't given proper learning opportunities, their enthusiasm for participating in knowledge-sharing can wane. Their ability to contribute valuable ideas might be limited when they lack adequate training and education. Also, without incentives or recognition mechanisms, employees might not feel motivated to engage in knowledge management. Some may not see the benefit of investing their time and effort in sharing expertise without some form of recognition.

3 - Strategies for Creating an Effective Knowledge Management System

3.1 - Identify Organizational Needs and Goals Pertinent to Knowledge

By conducting regular knowledge audits, organizations can assess the quality, relevance, and accessibility of their knowledge assets. These audits also help identify gaps, redundancies, or areas for improvement in the knowledge management system, ensuring that it aligns with the specific needs and objectives of the organization.

While conducting knowledge audits, organizations should also engage stakeholders at various departments and levels. This ensures a comprehensive understanding of the specific knowledge needs and goals across different areas of the organization. Through this process, organizations can prioritize knowledge initiatives and allocate resources effectively.

3.2 - Establish Clear Knowledge Policies and Framework

Organizations should implement clear policies and frameworks that govern data and information collection and utilization. These policies provide guidelines for maintaining consistency, ensuring compliance with regulations, and aligning with industry-specific standards. Moreover, a well-defined framework for knowledge management outlines the processes, roles, and responsibilities associated with various aspects of knowledge management in the company.

3.3 - Establish a Structured and Centralized Knowledge Management

Defining knowledge categories and taxonomies that are specific to your business processes and objectives is crucial. This structured framework will enable the effective capture, storage, and retrieval of knowledge, allowing employees to easily navigate and locate relevant information.

Besides defining categories and taxonomies, organizations should implement a knowledge repository. This repository can take the form of a digital platform or database that serves as a centralized hub for knowledge sharing and access. The repository should be user-friendly and searchable and support various content formats, such as documents, presentations, videos, and discussions.

Adopt technologies and tools that support knowledge management, such as knowledge bases, collaborative platforms, and artificial intelligence (AI) tools for knowledge discovery and recommendation. They can automate processes, facilitate knowledge sharing, and provide personalized recommendations to users, improving the effectiveness of knowledge management practices.

3.4 - Encourage and Facilitate Knowledge Sharing and Collaboration

Implement processes and tools that facilitate the capture and transfer of knowledge from subject experts to others. This can include documentation practices, knowledge transfer sessions, job rotation, forums, communities of practice, or mentorship programs.

Integrating knowledge sharing activities into project management processes is crucial. Project teams should be encouraged to document their experiences, best practices, and project-specific knowledge throughout the project lifecycle. This ensures that valuable knowledge is captured and can be applied in future projects.

To prevent knowledge loss when employees leave or transition to new roles, encouraging employees to document their expertise and even provide knowledge transfer sessions to fellow teammates is essential. This preservation of institutional knowledge facilitates its dissemination throughout the organization, ensuring continuity and preventing the loss of valuable insights.

Providing employees with the skills and support is essential. This includes offering training programs, user guides, and helpdesk services to address any technical or operational issues that may arise. Also, reward employees who actively contribute to the knowledge management system, acknowledging their valuable insights and active participation. By embedding knowledge sharing into daily practices and celebrating its importance, organizations create an environment where knowledge is valued and utilized to its maximum potential.

Conclusion

Realizing impactful knowledge utilization requires organizations to adopt a comprehensive and well-thought-out strategy. To unlock its full potential, organizations must actively foster a culture of knowledge sharing while also harnessing the right technology and tools to facilitate this process. Simultaneously, addressing the challenges that impede seamless knowledge exchange is paramount. As the business landscape keeps evolving at an unprecedented pace, the skill to effectively leverage knowledge is poised to stand as a cornerstone of success.

◆◆◆

Case Study

Navigating the Cosmos of Knowledge: Effective Knowledge Management at NASA

NASA's emphasis on knowledge sharing is driven by the critical nature of its missions and the complexities of its projects. Given the unique and pioneering work undertaken by the agency, a deep understanding of scientific and engineering principles, as well as operational intricacies amongst its staff, is paramount to its success. The stakes are high in space exploration, where even minor mistakes can have costly consequences. Within this specific context, the significance of knowledge sharing takes on a paramount role for NASA. The outstanding knowledge-sharing system that has emerged from their efforts presents a valuable subject of study for any organization aiming to refine and optimize its own strategies for knowledge management.

This significance of knowledge sharing is deeply ingrained in NASA's culture. The agency's unwavering commitment to fostering an open and collaborative environment enables solving complex challenges. With missions that push the boundaries of human capabilities, NASA understands that no single individual or team possesses all the expertise required. By promoting knowledge sharing, NASA unlocks the collective intelligence of its workforce.

However, like any other organization, NASA faces challenges in effectively managing its knowledge. One challenge is tackling the risk of knowledge loss because of employee turnover and retirement. Additionally, NASA's large and complex structure with multiple centers, disciplines, and projects can create knowledge silos and barriers. Moreover, the complexity of NASA's projects requires the development of effective methods and tools. In a rapidly changing environment, keeping the knowledge base up-to-date, relevant, and accurate is another challenge that demands continuous efforts in knowledge acquisition, creation, validation, updates, and curation.

Despite these challenges, NASA's exemplary commitment to effective knowledge management remains an inspiration. Systematic approaches to capture and transfer tacit knowledge are implemented to ensure continuity and prevent valuable insights from dissipating with departing employees. Learning from NASA's approach to knowledge sharing can serve as a blueprint for organizations seeking to harness the full potential of their workforce, push the boundaries of discovery, and achieve excellence in their respective fields. Let's delve into the enchanting mechanisms through which NASA achieves this feat!

Leadership Support

The unwavering commitment from its top leadership is a pivotal factor contributing to the resounding success of NASA's Knowledge Management (KM) system. The leaders at NASA provide the vision, strategic direction, well-defined goals, and clear objectives to drive the successful implementation of KM practices across the agency.

To further bolster its commitment, NASA has established a Chief Knowledge Officer (CKO) position at each of its centers and mission directorates. These CKOs play a crucial role in providing strategic direction and seamless coordination for all KM activities. Working closely with other senior leaders, they ensure that KM efforts align with the agency's overarching mission goals and priorities. This alignment facilitates the seamless integration of knowledge-sharing practices into NASA's core operations, maximizing the organization's potential for innovation and excellence.

In recognition of the multifaceted nature of KM, NASA has established a robust governance structure at various levels of the organization. This structure includes committees, councils, boards, and teams comprising experts and stakeholders who provide essential guidance, oversight, and decision-making on KM issues. Such governance mechanisms ensure that KM practices are robust and continuously evolving to meet the agency's dynamic challenges.

NASA's leadership has allocated substantial resources to support KM initiatives and practices to solidify their commitment further. By providing ample resources, NASA ensures that KM initiatives are well-funded, staffed with qualified personnel, and equipped with cutting-edge technology, optimizing their impact on the organization's overall success.

Organizational Culture

A pivotal factor contributing to this remarkably successful system is its strong organizational culture that places a high value on learning and innovation. One way NASA reinforces this culture is through several awards and recognition programs that acknowledge and reward employees for their contributions to KM. Moreover, NASA has created a robust learning environment that prioritizes continuous professional development for its employees. This environment encompasses various training, education, certification programs, and mentoring initiatives. By investing in their employees' growth and skills development, NASA ensures its workforce remains equipped with the latest competencies, enabling them to tackle complex challenges confidently.

An additional pivotal facet of their knowledge-sharing culture is its comprehensive array of policies, procedures, and guidelines that actively promote and incentivize employees to share their expertise, assets, and resources. This ethos of open communication and collaborative spirit forms an elemental cornerstone of NASA's Knowledge Management (KM) endeavors, profoundly contributing to the seamless circulation of knowledge across diverse teams, centers, and disciplines. In effect, this approach dismantles silos, fostering a culture of synergy and fostering cooperation that resonates throughout the organization.

KM Framework

A comprehensive and integrated KM framework serves as the guiding force behind NASA's knowledge management practices. It encompasses critical elements such as governance, strategy, processes, tools, metrics, roles, and competencies, working in tandem to optimize knowledge utilization across the organization.

NASA has developed a set of KM standards, guidelines, and best practices to maintain consistency and efficiency in managing its knowledge assets and flows. These serve as a common language and structured approach that ensures the highest levels of quality in all KM activities undertaken by the agency. By adhering to these standardized protocols, NASA maximizes the value of its knowledge resources and minimizes the risk of miscommunication or inefficiencies.

The framework also comprises a carefully formulated KM strategy, which outlines the vision, mission, goals, objectives, and initiatives driving the organization's KM efforts. By aligning KM activities with NASA's overarching organizational strategy and priorities, the KM strategy becomes an enabler of the agency's broader mission.

NASA's dedication to optimal knowledge management is further reinforced by a well-established set of processes that precisely defines the steps and procedures relevant to the capture and disbursement of critical knowledge. Through implementing these standardized processes, NASA orchestrates a harmonious knowledge-sharing ecosystem that facilitates the seamless execution of knowledge management practices on an expansive scale.

KM Practices

The crucial factor is its rich array of efficient KM practices. These practices are the backbone of capturing, sharing, transferring, and applying critical knowledge throughout the organization. Several exceptional practices include:

Knowledge Capture and Transfer (KCT):

KCT is a key strategy NASA uses to retain and preserve its critical knowledge. It means identifying, documenting, and transferring critical knowledge from departing or retiring employees to incoming or existing employees. By capturing the tacit knowledge of its experienced workforce and transferring it to the next generation, NASA mitigates the risks of knowledge loss and ensures the continuity of its critical operations.

KCT involves four steps:

- Identifying critical knowledge gaps and risks.
- Developing a KCT plan.
- Conducting KCT activities.

- Evaluating KCT outcomes

KCT activities include interviews, mentoring, coaching, shadowing, documentation, training, workshops, and webinars. It also uses tools such as Knowledge Maps, Knowledge Management Plans, and Knowledge Transfer Reports.

Illustrative Cases and Storytelling:

Case studies serve as a mechanism for capturing and disseminating insights gleaned from both successful and unsuccessful projects. These narratives encapsulate the day-to-day judgments and predicaments faced by managers within the realm of NASA, offering a potent learning resource for project management.

One way to capture and share tacit knowledge is by using stories to convey complex ideas, emotions, values, and culture simply and engagingly. Storytelling can be used for inspiring, motivating, teaching, and mentoring. NASA has several storytelling initiatives, such as the Masters with Masters series featuring interviews with experienced NASA leaders who share their stories and insights on various topics.

Federal Knowledge Community (FKC):

This assembly comprises a collective of adept knowledge management specialists from diverse federal agencies. Their collaborative efforts center around the exchange of strategies, hurdles, and remedies. The group convenes periodic sessions through webinars, workshops, conferences, and site visits. Additionally, they curate a comprehensive online platform offering a trove of knowledge management resources, encompassing articles, reports, presentations, podcasts, videos, and an array of other valuable assets.

Knowledge Sharing Workshop:

This interactive event gathers project teams or experts to exchange their insights on a specific topic or challenge. These workshops help capture lessons learned, find best practices, solve problems, generate ideas, share knowledge, and build relationships. Employing a spectrum of methodologies, including brainstorming, storytelling, after-action review (AAR), root cause analysis (RCA), and fishbone diagramming (Ishikawa), these sessions yield holistic and constructive outcomes.

Pause and Learn (PaL):

It is a straightforward yet impactful approach that empowers project teams to introspect about their achievements and setbacks. PaL entails taking deliberate breaks at crucial junctures or project phases to ponder over four fundamental questions: (1) What was supposed to happen? (2) What actually happened? (3) Why did it happen? (4) What can we do better next time?

Knowledge Management Plans (KMP):

This comprehensive dossier outlines the blueprint for a project's knowledge management strategy. It encompasses a roadmap of goals, objectives, actions, designated roles, obligations, resource allocations, performance metrics, and potential risks. KMP ensures that crucial knowledge is recognized and put into practice across the project's entire lifecycle.

Knowledge Maps:

This innovative knowledge management system adopts a visual approach, identifying and locating the sources of critical knowledge within an organization. They show relationships between knowledge domains, assets, holders, flows, gaps, and risks. Knowledge maps materialize through the expertise of KM practitioners or domain specialists, harnessed by utilizing mind mapping software, concept mapping software, and social network analysis software.

Knowledge Transfer Reports (KTR):

It is a document summarizing the results and outcomes of a KCT activity (Knowledge Capture and Transfer). KTR helps evaluate the effectiveness and impact of KCT on the recipient and the organization. It can include information such as the purpose of KCT, its method, its content, the feedback from participants, the lessons learned, and the recommendations for future KCT activities.

Shared Voyage:

A book capturing and sharing the insights gained from four remarkable projects: Advanced Composition Explorer (NASA), Joint Air-to-Surface Standoff Missile (U.S. Air Force), Pathfinder Solar-Powered Airplane (NASA), and Advanced Medium Range Air-to-Air Missile (U.S. Air Force). Shared Voyage provides insights into how these projects managed their challenges and achieved their successes through effective KM practices, such as leadership support, stakeholder engagement, risk management, innovation management, team building, and communication management.

Communities of Practice (CoP):

It is a group of people sharing a common interest or passion. They interact regularly to exchange knowledge, experiences, and ideas. CoP can be formal or informal, internal or external, local or global, face-to-face or virtual, and provide a platform for learning, networking, collaborating, innovating, and mentoring. NASA has several CoPs on project management, systems engineering, software engineering, safety, and mission assurance.

Knowledge Services:

This integral division caters to the organizational need for comprehensive KM support and services. Knowledge services include KM planning, training, consulting, facilitation, evaluation, research, and communication. Knowledge services can be provided by a dedicated KM team or by a cross-functional KM network. NASA has several knowledge service units, such as the Academy of Program/Project & Engineering Leadership (APPEL), the Office of the Chief Knowledge Officer (OCKO), and the Office of the Chief Engineer (OCE).

Knowledge Management Metrics:

This is a set of measures evaluating the performance and impact of KM initiatives and practices on the organization. These can include quantitative metrics such as usage statistics, satisfaction ratings, cost savings, revenue growth, productivity improvement, or innovation rate, as well as qualitative metrics such as success stories, testimonials, case studies, proven approaches, and lessons learned. KM metrics can be collected and analyzed using surveys, interviews, focus groups, observation, and benchmarking.

Lessons Learned:

A database or repository capturing lessons from past projects or experiences. Lessons learned can be used for improving project performance, avoiding past mistakes, replicating past achievements, and transferring knowledge. NASA maintains a lessons-learned database containing over 1,000 records on various critical topics.

Ensuring Quality and Accuracy

NASA places great importance on maintaining the quality and accuracy of its vast knowledge assets. To achieve this, the organization employs a range of approaches and strategies, ensuring that its knowledge remains reliable and up-to-date. Some practical measures include:

Peer Review:

NASA implements a meticulous peer review process where subject experts thoroughly review the content of knowledge resources such as technical reports, research papers, and conference proceedings. Internal or external experts conduct the peer review using standardized tools such as review checklists and feedback forms. This ensures the information is high quality, accurate, relevant, and comprehensive.

Validation:

To ascertain the practical applicability and effectiveness of its knowledge assets, NASA conducts thorough validation procedures. It validates important tools, methods, processes, and standards to ensure they meet the organization's exacting standards. Project teams or end-users test and verify in real-world scenarios using tools such as pilot projects, prototypes, simulations, and experiments. This process ensures that the knowledge derived from various sources is reliable and can be successfully applied to real-life situations.

Update:

Understanding the dynamic nature of knowledge, NASA actively updates and revises the content of its knowledge assets to reflect the latest advancements in various domains. Knowledge owners or KM practitioners play a vital role in this process, using update schedules, logs, and notifications to ensure timely updates. By keeping its policies, procedures, guidelines, handbooks, and other resources up-to-date, NASA ensures its workforce access accurate and relevant information.

Curation:

NASA adopts a meticulous curation process to systematically organize and manage its knowledge assets. This ensures that the information remains usable and discoverable by its workforce. Knowledge practitioners and information professionals use metadata, taxonomy, indexing, and archiving standards to optimize the organization's knowledge resources. This way NASA maintains a wealth of valuable information ready for use when needed.

Conclusion

NASA's effective knowledge management stems from several factors: leadership support, organizational culture, KM framework, and KM practices. By systematically coordinating and leveraging these factors, it boosts its organizational learning and performance. The agency's ability to tap into collective intelligence has led to groundbreaking discoveries, technological advances, and successful space missions.

NASA showcases successful knowledge management on a large scale, and other organizations can certainly apply similar approaches and strategies in their own contexts.

◆◆◆

Epilogue

Congratulations on reaching the final chapter of this book! Throughout this journey, we have delved into the key components that contribute to creating a culture of excellence within an organization. In these pages, we have thoroughly explored various aspects of establishing and sustaining a high-performance organization. We have examined how people, culture, leadership, change management, agility, continuous improvement, and knowledge/information management all play pivotal roles in constructing such an organization. Let us now consolidate the essential points covered in the book below:

The Role of People and Culture in Building HPOs

It has been understood that establishing a positive and inclusive culture plays a pivotal role in building a high-performance workforce. Organizations that prioritize employee development and invest in their well-being have a higher chance of achieving their goals. Overall, it is of utmost importance to create a people-centric culture.

The Importance of Leadership in HPOs

Effective leadership is vital to building a high-performance organization. Leaders should have the right characteristics, such as being visionary, inspiring, and able to motivate their teams. Additionally, they must establish the organization's strategic trajectory and possess the capacity to make pivotal decisions even in situations marked by uncertainty and high pressure. Organizations that have strong leaders can better navigate challenges and drive performance.

Change Management in HPOs

Change is a constant in today's fast-paced business environment, and HPOs need to be adaptable and open to change. For effective change management, organizations should establish a robust infrastructure, cultivate a skilled and resilient workforce, and establish effective communication channels. Engaging employees in the change process becomes imperative to ensure seamless implementation and ultimately achieve success.

Speedy Agility in HPOs

HPOs should be able to respond quickly to changing market conditions and customer needs. They need to foster experimentation, risk-taking, and innovation. Employees should be encouraged to embrace change, think outside the box, and constantly look for new ways to improve performance.

Continuous Improvement in HPOs

Organizations should continuously strive to improve their processes, products, and services. This requires a commitment to ongoing learning and development and a culture that encourages feedback and constructive criticism. Leaders should be in frontline to promote such a learning-oriented culture and empower their team members to make decisions that drive the organization forward.

Knowledge/Information Management in HPOs

To enhance performance, organizations must harness knowledge and information effectively. It's crucial to guarantee that employees can readily access the information necessary for their roles. Organizations should foster a culture of knowledge-sharing and collaboration, harness technology efficiently, motivate employees to contribute their insights and skills, and acknowledge those who make meaningful contributions to the organization's achievements.

As we draw near the culmination of this book, I want to emphasize a resounding call to action. It is not enough to simply understand the principles and strategies discussed here; it is time to take action and implement them within your organization. Reflect on the principles outlined and assess where your organization currently stands.

Are you leveraging the power of your people? Do you possess a culture that is oriented towards achieving results and fostering growth? Do you have leaders who inspire and drive change? Are you actively striving to foster continuous improvement and innovation? Let these questions serve as guiding lights as you embark on the transformative journey of constructing a high-performance organization.

Commit yourself to the vision of becoming a high-performance organization, demonstrating unwavering dedication, perseverance, and a willingness to make necessary sacrifices. Engage your leaders and employees actively in this transformative process. Educate them on the principles of high-performance organizations and involve them in the development of the implementation strategy and action plan. Foster an environment of open communication and collaboration, empowering your employees to take ownership of their work.

Furthermore, it is crucial to stay agile and adaptable in the face of a constant change in the business landscape. High-performance organizations are those that can swiftly respond to emerging challenges and seize new opportunities. Embrace change as an impetus for growth, encourage innovation, and remain receptive to fresh ideas. Learn from failures encountered along the journey, and celebrate the successes achieved along the way.

Remember, building a consistently high performing organization is not a onetime event; it is an ongoing journey. Continuously monitor your progress, gather feedback, and make adjustments as needed. Strive for excellence in everything you do, and never settle for mediocrity.

I challenge you to be one of the few organizations that reach the summit of high performance. Embrace the principles and strategies outlined in this book, allowing them to serve as your compass on the path to realizing your vision. The road ahead may be steep, and the obstacles may be many, but with determination, perseverance, and a commitment to excellence, you can achieve remarkable results. Now is the time to take action. I believe in your potential, and I am confident that you can succeed.

On behalf of all the contributors to this book, I extend my sincerest wishes for your success on your journey toward creating a top-performing company. May your commitment, drive, and unwavering pursuit of excellence inspire others within your organization and beyond. Remember, the sky is not the limit when it comes to achieving high performance – it is just the beginning of what you and your organization can accomplish!

About The Author

Surbhi R. Bhosle is a content writer specializing in the field of Business and Human Resources (HR), with six years of experience in this dynamic industry. She holds Master's Degree in Human Resources and has cultivated a wealth of experience collaborating with a diverse clientele. Her contributions to their blogs are characterized by well-researched, in-depth articles that primarily delve into the intricate realm of human resources and the nuances involved in building high-performance organizations.

Beyond her writing prowess, Surbhi brings firsthand corporate experience, having served as a systems engineer in a prestigious IT firm for nearly two years. This practical insight into the corporate world adds a unique layer to her understanding of human resources, organizational culture, and strategic management.

Surbhi's journey and insights have led her to pen her latest work, 'The High Performance Blueprint – Strategies for Sustainable Success in Modern Organizations.' Her motivation behind this book is clear: to equip readers with practical guidance and profound insights into the mindset and behaviors essential for fostering a culture of high performance within organizations.

Her writing style is characterized by its clarity, conciseness, and accessibility, making the book an invaluable resource for anyone on the quest to build a high-performance organization. Surbhi's profound knowledge and her unwavering passion for assisting organizations in their pursuit of success establish her as a trusted authority in this field.

Note From the Author:

Dear Reader,

I extend my heartfelt gratitude for immersing yourself in my book. Your thoughts and feedback hold immense value to me. If this book has been insightful or helpful to you in any way, I would greatly appreciate it if you could share your review. Your reviews will help others discover this work and would really mean the world to me!

Visit https://mybook.to/HPOBlueprint to leave your review.

Thank you once again for being part of this journey and for all your support.

Warm regards,

Surbhi

References

Chapter 1

1.1. 2023 Gen Z and Millennial Survey (deloitte.com)

Available From: https://www.deloitte.com/global/en/about/press-room/2023-gen-z-and-millenial-survey.html

1.2. On the cusp of adulthood and facing an uncertain future: what we know about gen-z so far

Available From: https://www.pewresearch.org/social-trends/2020/05/14/on-the-cusp-of-adulthood-and-facing-an-uncertain-future-what-we-know-about-gen-z-so-far-2/

1.3. Statistics on Workplace Harassment 2021 | AllVoices

Available From: https://www.allvoices.co/blog/the-state-of-workplace-harassment-2021

1.4. What Is Customer Engagement? Key Findings from Global Research To Help Your Business Grow

Available From: https://www.salesforce.com/resources/articles/customer-engagement/

1.5. André de Waal MSc, MBA, PhD - HPO Center

Available From: https://www.hpocenter.com/hpo-expert/andre-de-waal-msc-mba-phd/

1.6. The High Performance Organization (HPO) Framework - HPO Center

Available From: https://www.hpocenter.com/hpo-framework/

1.7. Different Motivations for Different Generations of Workers

Available From: https://www.inc.com/john-rampton/different-motivations-for-different-generations-of-workers-boomers-gen-x-millennials-gen-z.html

1.8. Common Characteristics of the Traditionalists Generation

Available From: https://www.thebalancecareers.com/workplace-characteristics-silent-generation-2164692

1.9. Overgeneralizing the generations

Available From: https://www.apa.org/monitor/2009/06/workplaces

1.10. From Baby Boomers to Generation Z

Available From: https://www.psychologytoday.com/us/blog/the-truisms-wellness/201602/baby-boomers-generation-z

1.11. Millennials at work: five stereotypes - and why they are (mostly) wrong

Available From: https://www.theguardian.com/world/2016/mar/15/millennials-work-five-stereotypes-generation-y-jobs

1.12. Guide to Gen Z: Debunking the Myths of Our Youngest Generation

Available From: https://www.npd.com/news/thought-leadership/2018/guide-to-gen-z-debunking-the-myths-of-our-youngest-generation/

1.13. From Baby Boomers to Generation Z

Available From: https://www.psychologytoday.com/us/blog/the-truisms-wellness/201602/baby-boomers-generation-z

1.14. Social Construction of the Value–Behaviour Relation

Available From: https://www.ncbi.nlm.nih.gov/pmc/articles/PMC6504687/

1.15. 8 Common Baby Boomer Characteristics in the Workplace

Available From: https://www.indeed.com/career-advice/finding-a-job/baby-boomer-characteristics

1.16. Generational Differences in the Workplace – Explained

Available From: https://www.4cornerresources.com/blog/generational-differences- in-the-workplace/

1.17. 11 Common Characteristics of the Silent Generation

Available From: https://www.indeed.com/career-advice/career-development/characteristics-of-silent-generation

1.18. Silent Generation

Available From: https://www.britannica.com/topic/Silent-Generation

1.19. Generational Differences in the Workplace

Available From: https://www.purdueglobal.edu/education-partnerships/generational-workforce-differences-infographic/

1.20. What Is Generation X? (Characteristics and Careers

Available From: https://ca.indeed.com/career-advice/career-development/generation-x-characteristics

1.21. Leading the Four Generations at Work

Available From: https://www.https://www.amanet.org/articles/leading-the-four-generations-at-work/.org/articles/leading-the-four-generations-at-work

1.22. 10 Common Characteristics of the Millennial Generation

Available From: https://www.indeed.com/career-advice/interviewing/10-millennial-generation-characteristics

1.23. Managing Millennials in the Workplace

Available From: https://www.businessnewsdaily.com/15974-millennials-in-the-workplace.html

1.24. The Millennial Generation—Birth Years, Characteristics, and History

Available From: https://www.familysearch.org/en/blog/millennial-generation

1.25. 7 Characteristics about Generation Z in the Workplace

Available From: https://www.indeed.com/career-advice/finding-a-job/generation-z

1.26. What is Gen Z

Available From: https://www.mckinsey.com/featured-insights/mckinsey-explainers/what-is-gen-z

1.27. Can 5 Generations Coexist In The Workplace

Available From: https://www.forbes.com/sites/jackkelly/2023/03/01/can-five-generations-coexist-in-the-workplace/?sh=1188599431f2

Chapter 2

2.1. Attracting and Retaining the Right Talent

Available From: https://www.mckinsey.com/capabilities/people-and-organizational-performance/our-insights/attracting-and-retaining-the-right-talent

2.2. Why Your Employer Brand Matters - Whitepaper | LinkedIn

Available From: https://business.linkedin.com/content/dam/business/talent-solutions/global/en_US/site/pdf/datasheets/linkedin-why-your-employer-brand-matters-en-us.pdf

2.3. Glassdoor

https://www.glassdoor.co.in/index.htm

2.4. Zappos' New Recruiting Strategy Seen as Innovative, Risky (shrm.org)

Available From: https://www.shrm.org/ResourcesAndTools/hr-topics/talent-acquisition/Pages/Zappos-Job-Posts.aspx

2.5. Inside Zappos (@InsideZappos) / Twitter

Available From: https://twitter.com/InsideZappos

2.6. Zappos Culture – Instagram

Available From: https://www.instagram.com/zapposculture/

2.7. Zappos Stories - Youtube

https://www.youtube.com/channel/UCHGPRPNUKtjsE5RFSOMLVoQ

2.8. HackerRank

https://www.hackerrank.com/

2.9. Codility

https://www.codility.com/

2.10. LinkedIn Recruiter

https://business.linkedin.com/en-in/talent-solutions/recruiter

2.11. About Us | Zappos.com

Available From: https://www.zappos.com/c/about

2.12. How We Work | Zappos.com

Available From: https://www.zappos.com/about/how-we-work

2.13. Zappos Insights

Available From: https://www.zappos.com/c/zappos-insights

2.14. Zappos Internship

Available From: Zappos College Internship Program | Zappos.com Culture Blog

2.15. Virtual Culture Book

Available From: https://www.zappos.com/c/zappos-insights-contact?pf_rd_r=3X3DDT180ZDHVF1FTAKQ&pf_rd_p=79769bf5-3622-4de5-98a2-aeb4b106e5e5

2.16. What We Live By | Zappos.com

Available From: https://www.zappos.com/about/what-we-live-by

2.17. Zappos ONE - Our Circles | Zappos.com

Available From: https://www.zappos.com/c/zappos-one-circles?pf_rd_r=TY37DV61WNW6EGYZMC61&pf_rd_p=b99794db-faa2-4e92-8147-7829ed082e32#:~:text=Zappos%20Asians%20and%20Pacific%20Islanders%20Circle

2.18. Zappos ONE | Zappos.com

Available From: https://www.zappos.com/c/zappos-one?pf_rd_r=VV88B52P24EEVQ69HCR6&pf_rd_p=82302d09-00d3-4468-a91b-e35dde7363b4

2.19. Zappos' Employee Experience Unleashed

Available from: https://www.freshworks.com/hrms/zappos-employee-experience-blog/

2.20. Zappos| Business Insider India

Available From: https://www.businessinsider.in/strategy/news/zappos-gives-new-employees-4-weeks-to-decide-if-its-a-good-fit-and-lets-them-quit-with-pay-if-not-their-head-of-hr-explains-how-this-policy-has-helped-them-save-money-and-hire-great-people-/articleshow/72129137.cms

2.21. Zappos Insights | Zappos.com

Available From: https://www.zappos.com/c/zappos-insights

2.22. Inside a Zappos Employee Meeting: 11 Things You Won't See at Any Other Company

Available From: https://www.bizbash.com/venues-destinations/united-states/las-vegas/article/13231506/inside-a-zappos-employee-meeting-11-things-you-wont-see-at anyothercompany#:~:text=The%20Zappos%20quarterly%20"all%20hands,as%20lots%20of%20quirky%20touches

2.23. How Zappos Designs Culture Using Core Values

Available From: https://www.fearlessculture.design/blog-posts/zappos-culture-design-canvas

2.24. Zappos gets savvy with social media | Reuters.com

Available From: https://www.reuters.com/article/urnidgns002570f3005978d8852576540053f02b-idUS280016341920091019

2.25. Creating a Memorable Onboarding Experience | Zappos Stories - YouTube

Available From: https://www.youtube.com/watch?v=zD2SVwXMYHA

2.26. How Zappos Onboards New Hires Weirdly (but Effectively): Detailed Breakdown & Tips

Available From: https://www.zavvy.io/hr-examples/employee-onboarding-at-zappos

2.27. Diversity & Inclusion In The Workplace - Zappos ONE | Zappos Stories – YouTube

Available From: https://www.youtube.com/watch?v=FOJQDtCoXcQ

2.28. A Motivating Place to Work: The Case of Zappos–Organizational Behavior

Available From: https://open.lib.umn.edu/organizationalbehavior/chapter/5-1-a-motivating-place-to-work-the-case-of-zappos/

2.29. Find Out the Ways Zappos Reinforces Its Company Culture (liveabout.com

Available From: https://www.liveabout.com/zappos-company-culture-1918813

2.30. Zappos – Hiring for Culture and the Bizarre Things They Do (zippia.com

Available From: https://www.zippia.com/employer/zappos-hiring-for-culture-and-the-bizarre-things-they-do/

2.31. Zappos Case Study

Available From: https://subjecto.com/essay-samples/zappos-case-study/

2.32. Zappos: Proving The Power Employer Branding

Available From: https://softgarden.com/en/blog/zappos-proving-power-employer-branding/

2.33. Zappos - Deloitte US

Available From: https://www2.deloitte.com/content/dam/insights/us/articles/zappos/DUP345_Case-Study_Zappos_vFINAL.pdf

2.34. Inspiring Case Studies for Companies Looking To Transform Their Employer Brand

Available from: https://www.forbes.com/sites/kimberlywhitler/2021/06/15/inspiring-case-studies-for-companies-looking-to-transform-their-employer-brand/

2.35. How Zappos Uses Social Media for Recruiting - Business News Daily

Available From: https://www.businessnewsdaily.com/10567-zappos-social-media-recruiting.html

2.36. The Zappos Holacracy Experiment (hbr.org

Available From: https://hbr.org/podcast/2016/07/the-zappos-holacracy-experiment

2.37. Home - The Valuable 500

Available From: https://www.thevaluable500.com/

2.38. Zappos.com Joins Valuable 500 and Reinforces Commitment to Disability Inclusion

Available From: https://www.prnewswire.com/news-releases/zapposcom-joins-valuable-500-and-reinforces-commitment-to-disability-inclusion-301278012.html

2.39. Employer branding on LinkedIn

Available From: https://indiafreenotes.com/employer-branding-on-linkedin/

2.40. 10 awesome employer brands (and what makes them great

Available From: https://www.workstars.com/recognition-and-engagement-blog/2020/02/27/10-awesome-employer-brands-and-what-makes-them-great/

Chapter 3

3.1. Microsoft rides Azure, cloud commercial revenue in strong Q4 | ZDNET

Available From: https://Chaswww.zdnet.com/article/microsoft-rides-azure-cloud-commercial-revenue-in-strong-q4/

3.2. Cloud revenues power Microsoft's $51.7 billion Q2 in fiscal year 2022 | ZDNET

Available From: https://www.zdnet.com/article/microsoft-cloud-revenues-power-microsofts-51-7-billion-second-fy22-quarter/

3.3. FY22 Q4 - Press Releases - Investor Relations - Microsoft

Available From: https://www.microsoft.com/en-us/Investor/earnings/FY-2022-Q4/press-release-webcast

3.4. Racial Equity Initiative: A year of progress on our commitments - The Official Microsoft Blog

Available From: https://blogs.microsoft.com/blog/2021/06/21/racial-equity-initiative-a-year-of-progress-on-our-commitments/

3.5. Microsoft will be carbon negative by 2030

Available From: https://blogs.microsoft.com/blog/2020/01/16/microsoft-will-be-carbon-negative-by-2030/

3.6. AI Platform, Products & Tools - Microsoft AI

Available From: https://www.microsoft.com/en-us/ai/ai-platform

3.7. Ai (microsoft.com)

Available From: https://azure.microsoft.com/en-in/solutions/ai/

3.8. Artificial Intelligence - Getting Started with Microsoft AI | Microsoft Learn

Available From: https://learn.microsoft.com/en-us/archive/msdn-magazine/2017/connect/artificial-intelligence-getting-started-with-microsoft-ai

3.9. Microsoft and OpenAI extend partnership - The Official Microsoft Blog

Available From: https://blogs.microsoft.com/blog/2023/01/23/microsoftandopenaiextendpartnership/

3.10. LinkedIn in Microsoft apps and services - Microsoft Support

Available From: https://support.microsoft.com/en-us/office/linkedin-in-microsoft-apps-and-services-6d7c5b09-d525-424a-9c18-8081ee7a67e8

3.11. Microsoft and Open Source: An unofficial timeline

Available From: https://boxofcables.dev/microsoft-and-open-source-an-unofficial-timeline/

3.12. Racial Equity Initiative | Microsoft

Available From: https://www.microsoft.com/en-us/racial-equity-initiative?activetab=pivot1%3aprimaryr2

3.13. Microsoft and U.S. Department of Commerce Help Minority- and Women-Owned Businesses Unlock Potential - Stories

Available From: https://news.microsoft.com/2005/05/23/microsoft-and-u-s-department-of-commerce-help-minority-and-women-owned-businesses-unlock-potential/

3.14. Microsoft goes live with the Microsoft Sustainability manager at the Summit of Americas

Available From: https://news.microsoft.com/es-xl/microsoft-goes-live-with-the-microsoft-sustainability-manager-at-the-summit-of-americas/

3.15. Connect to the Emissions Impact Dashboard for Azure - Power BI | Microsoft Learn

Available From: https://learn.microsoft.com/en-us/power-bi/connect-data/service-connect-to-emissions-impact-dashboard

3.16. Cloud for Sustainability API (preview) overview - Microsoft Cloud for Sustainability | Microsoft Learn

Available From: https://learn.microsoft.com/en-us/industry/sustainability/api-overview

3.17. Introducing the latest ESG innovations with Microsoft Cloud for Sustainability - Microsoft Industry Blogs

Available From: https://www.microsoft.com/en-us/industry/blog/sustainability/2023/06/15/introducing-the-latest-esg-innovations-with-microsoft-cloud-for-sustainability/

3.18. Accelerate your journey to net-zero with Microsoft Cloud for Sustainability - Microsoft Industry Blogs

Available From: https://www.microsoft.com/en-us/industry/blog/sustainability/2022/06/01/accelerate-your-journey-to-net-zero-with-microsoft-cloud-for-sustainability/

3.19. Microsoft Future Ready: Industry leaders call for recalibrating businesses to embrace digital-first India - Microsoft Stories India

Available From: https://news.microsoft.com/en-in/microsoft-future-ready-industry-leaders-call-for-recalibrating-businesses-to-embrace-digital-first-india/

3.20. People-Centric Technology - Microsoft Industry Blogs - Canada

Available From: https://www.microsoft.com/en-ca/industry/blog/uncategorized/2017/03/27/people-centric-technology/

3.21. Satya Nadella promises customers a 'people-centric IT' - CNET

Available From: https://www.cnet.com/tech/tech-industry/satya-nadella-promises-customers-a-people-centric-it/

3.22. Microsoft CEO Satya Nadella is the most successful CEO of the Tech industry

Available From: https://ceoworld.biz/2022/03/24/microsoft-ceo-satya-nadella-is-the-most-successful-ceo-of-tech-industry/

3.23. How Satya Nadella brought a growth mindset to Microsoft | Mint (livemint.com

Available From: https://www.livemint.com/news/business-of-life/how-satya-nadella-brought-a-growth-mindset-to-microsoft-11614874643362.html

3.24. Satya Nadella's Simple Framework for Clear, Concise Communication (forbes.com

Available From: https://www.forbes.com/sites/carminegallo/2023/01/25/satya-nadellas-simple-framework-for-clear-concise-communication/?sh=4df9ebaa3ac3

3.25. Addressing racial injustice - The Official Microsoft Blog

Available From: https://blogs.microsoft.com/blog/2020/06/23/addressing-racial-injustice/

3.26. Microsoft and OpenAI extend partnership - The Official Microsoft Blog

Available From: https://blogs.microsoft.com/blog/2023/01/23/microsoftandopenaiextendpartnership/

3.27. Microsoft to Invest $10 Billion in ChatGPT Maker OpenAI (MSFT) - Bloomberg

Available From: https://www.bloomberg.com/news/articles/2023-01-23/microsoft- makes-multibillion-dollar-investment-in-openai

3.28. Microsoft invests in and partners with OpenAI to support us building beneficial AGI

Available From: https://openai.com/blog/microsoft-invests-in-and-partners-with-openai

3.29. Satya Nadella's focus on growth mindset explored in "Hit Refresh"

Available From: https://www.avanade.com/en/blogs/avanade-insights/business-of-technology/satya-nadella-hit-refresh

3.30. Satya Nadella Lays out a Vision for Microsoft at Ignite 2021...What it Means for the Company & the Cloud

Available From: https://wikibon.com/breaking-analysis-satya-nadella-lays-out-a-vision-for-microsoft-at-ignite-2021-what-it-means-for-the-company-the-cloud/

3.31. In Satya Nadella's future vision, cloud to help all firms build own tech

Available From: https://www.hindustantimes.com/business-news/in-satya-nadella-s-future-vision-cloud-to-help-all-firms-build-own-tech/story-zE4dFezjD1O40EvKH8HFzN.html

3.32. How Satya Nadella Sees Future of the Cloud

Available From: https://www.businessinsider.com/microsoft-satya-nadella-future-cloud-five-attributes-2021-3

3.33. Read Microsoft CEO's memo to staff about LinkedIn acquisition

Available From: https://www.theverge.com/2016/6/13/11920306/microsoft-ceo-satya-nadella-linkedin-memo

3.34. Why is Microsoft buying LinkedIn? CEO Satya Nadella explains in memo to employees. Full Text

Available From: https://www.indiatoday.in/technology/news/story/why-is-microsoft-buying-linkedin-ceo-satya-nadella-explains-in-memo-to-employees-full-text-13948-2016-06-13

3.35. Microsoft's Satya Nadella outlines vision on LinkedIn integration

Available From: https://indianexpress.com/article/technology/tech-news-technology/satya-nadella-outlines-microsofts-vision-on-linkedin-integration-following-acquisition-4418640/

3.36. Microsoft Corporate Social Responsibility

Available From: https://www.microsoft.com/en-us/corporate-responsibility/sustainability

3.37. Sustainability: A year of progress and a decade of action

Available From: https://blogs.microsoft.com/on-the-issues/2021/01/28/sustainability-year-progress-decade-action/

3.38. Capitalism 'will fundamentally be in jeopardy' if business does not act on climate change, Microsoft CEO Satya Nadella says

Available From: https://www.cnbc.com/2020/01/16/microsoft-ceo-capitalism-is-in-jeopardy-if-we-do-not-act-on-climate-change.html

3.39. Progress on our goal to be carbon negative by 2030

Available From: https://blogs.microsoft.com/on-the-issues/2020/07/21/carbon-negative-transform-to-net-zero/

3.40. Satya Nadella - Chairman and Chief Executive Officer

Available From: https://news.microsoft.com/exec/satya-nadella/

3.41. Microsoft Inspire 2021 Satya Nadella

Available From: https://news.microsoft.com/wp-content/uploads/prod/2021/07/Microsoft-Inspire-2021-Satya-Nadella.pdf

3.42. In First Person: Satya Nadella

Available From: https://www.shrm.org/executive/resources/people-strategy-journal/fall2020/pages/in-first-person.aspx

3.43. Microsoft CEO Satya Nadella: Finding Success Out Of The Spotlight

Available From: https://www.forbes.com/sites/grantfreeland/2019/03/18/microsoft-ceo-satya-nadellas-success-secret/

3.44. How An Obsession with Customers Made Microsoft A Two-Trillion Dollar Company

Available From: https://www.forbes.com/sites/stevedenning/2021/06/25/how-customers-made-microsoft-a-two-trillion-dollar-company/

3.45. Satya Nadella is All About Customer Focus, Employee Engagement, and Changing the World

Available From: https://jdmeier.com/satya-nadella-is-all-about-customer-focus/

3.46. Diversity and Inclusion | Microsoft

Available From: https://www.microsoft.com/en-us/diversity/default.aspx

3.47. Microsoft CEO Satya Nadella says $7.5 billion GitHub deal shows, 'We are all in on open source'

Available From: https://www.cnbc.com/2018/06/04/microsoft-ceo-satya-nadella-on-github-we-are-all-in-on-open-source.html

3.48. The CEO who will run Microsoft's $7.5 billion bet on open source explains the vision for leading a software revolution it spent years fighting

Available From: https://www.businessinsider.com/github-ceo-nat-friedman-microsoft-satya-nadella-open-source-2018-10

3.49. How Satya Nadella brought Microsoft back from irrelevancy

Available From: https://www.newsbytesapp.com/news/business/the-transformation-of-microsoft-under-satya-nadella/story

3.50. Microsoft's Satya Nadella on Flexible Work, the Metaverse, and the Power of Empathy

Available From: https://hbr.org/2021/10/microsofts-satya-nadella-on-flexible-work-the-metaverse-and-the-power-of-empathy

3.51. What is Satya Nadella's strategy for Microsoft?

Available From: https://www.techradar.com/news/world-of-tech/what-is-satya-nadella-s-strategy-for-microsoft-1222212

3.52. How Satya Nadella overhauled Microsoft's cutthroat culture and turned it into a trillion-dollar 'growth mindset' company

Available From: https://www.businessinsider.in/tech/news/case-study-how-satya-nadella-overhauled-microsofts-cutthroat-culture-and-turned-it-into-a-trillion-dollar-growth-mindset-company/articleshow/74466098.cms

3.53. Microsoft launches new AI Skills Initiative and grant

Available From: https://news.microsoft.com/en-in/microsoft-launches-new-ai-skills-initiative-and-grant/

3.54. Microsoft Hypergrowth: Beyond Azure, Satya Nadella's 5 Superstars

Available From: https://accelerationeconomy.com/cloud/microsoft-hypergrowth-beyond-azure-satya-nadellas-5-superstars/

3.55. Microsoft CEO Satya Nadella's Plan to Unlock 'Trillions of Dollars' In Partner Opportunity

Available From: https://www.crn.com/news/cloud/microsoft-ceo-satya-nadella-s-plan-to-unlock-trillions-of-dollars-in-partner-opportunity

3.56. We're building Azure as the world's computer: Satya Nadella

Available From: https://news.microsoft.com/en-in/features/building-azure-as-the-worlds-computer-satya-nadella/

3.57. Satya Nadella Remade Microsoft as World's Most Valuable Company - Bloomberg

Available From: https://www.bloomberg.com/news/features/2019-05-02/satya-nadella-remade-microsoft-as-world-s-most-valuable-company

3.58. Microsoft's LinkedIn Acquisition: Taking over the professional world | LinkedIn

Available From: https://www.linkedin.com/pulse/microsofts-linkedin-acquisition-taking-over-world-prachi-tyagi/

3.59. Microsoft vows to use financial strength to fuel societal change in sweeping racial justice plan – GeekWire

Available From: https://www.geekwire.com/2020/microsoft-vows-use-financial-strength-fuel-societal-change-sweeping-racial-justice-plan/

3.60. Chart: Big Three Dominate the Global Cloud Market | Statista

Available From: https://www.statista.com/chart/18819/worldwide-market-share-of-leading-cloud-infrastructure-service-providers/

3.61. Microsoft's 2021 Diversity & Inclusion report: Demonstrating progress and remaining accountable to our commitments - The Official Microsoft Blog

Available From: https://blogs.microsoft.com/blog/2021/10/20/microsofts-2021-diversity-inclusion-report-demonstrating-progress-and-remaining-accountable-to-our-commitments/

3.62. Progress on our goal to be carbon negative by 2030 - Microsoft On the Issues

Available From: https://blogs.microsoft.com/on-the-issues/2020/07/21/carbon-negative-transform-to-net-zero/

3.63. Sustainability: A year of progress and a decade of action - Microsoft on the Issues

Available From: https://blogs.microsoft.com/on-the-issues/2021/01/28/sustainability-year-progress-decade-action/

3.64. Microsoft Sustainability Manager overview | Microsoft Learn

Available From: https://learn.microsoft.com/en-us/industry/sustainability/sustainability-manager-overview

3.65. 2022 Environmental Sustainability Report | Microsoft CSR

Available From: https://www.microsoft.com/en-us/corporate-responsibility/sustainability/report

3.66. Calculating My Carbon Footprint | Microsoft Sustainability

Available From: https://www.microsoft.com/en-us/ sustainability/emissions-impact-dashboard

3.67. Microsoft is rolling out a new management framework to its leaders. It centers around a psychological insight called growth mindset. | Business Insider India

Available From: https://www.businessinsider.in/strategy/news/microsoft-is-rolling-out-a-new-management-framework-to-its-leaders-it-centers-around-a-psychological-insight-called-growth-mindset-/articleshow/72014938.cms

3.68. How did Satya Nadella Instill a Growth Mindset at Microsoft? | by Bhavya Siddappa | Medium

Available From: https://bhavis.medium.com/how-did-satya-nadella-instill-a-growth-mindset-at-microsoft-f500fb9805c0

3.69. What is Microsoft Cloud for Sustainability? | Microsoft Learn

Available From: https://learn.microsoft.com/en-us/industry/sustainability/overview

Chapter 4

4.1. The powerful role financial incentives can play in a transformation - McKinsey Available From: https://www.mckinsey.com/capabilities/transformation/our-insights/the-powerful-role-financial-incentives-can-play-in-a-transformation

4.2. 2022 Inclusion Report Update - About Netflix

Available From: https://about.netflix.com/en/news/2022-inclusion-report-update

4.3. Netflix Adds 9 Million Subscribers in Third Quarter - The New York Times (nytimes.com)

Available From: https://www.nytimes.com/2023/10/18/business/media/netflix-earnings.html

4.4. This is how Netflix's top-secret recommendation system works | WIRED UK

Available From: https://www.wired.co.uk/article/how-do-netflixs-algorithms-work-machine-learning-helps-to-predict-what-viewers-will-like

4.5. How Netflix Reinvented HR (hbr.org)

Available From: https://hbr.org/2014/01/how-netflix-reinvented-hr

4.6. History of Netflix: Timeline and Facts - TheStreet

Available From: https://www.thestreet.com/technology/history-of-netflix-15091518

4.7. How and When Did Netflix Start? A Brief History of the Company (makeuseof.com)

Available From: https://www.makeuseof.com/how-when-netflix-start-brief-company-history/

4.8. Netflix Jobs

Available From: https://jobs.netflix.com/inclusion

4.9. Netflix Culture – Seeking Excellence

Available From: https://jobs.netflix.com/culture

4.10. IRJET-V7I4306.pdf

Available From: https://www.irjet.net/archives/V7/i4/IRJET-V7I4306.pdf

4.11. Netflix Change Management Analysis & Solution

Available From: http://fernfortuniversity.com/hbr/change-management/15138-netflix-blockbuster.php

4.12. Netflix Change Management Case Study

Available From: https://changemanagementinsight.com/netflix-change-management-case-study/

4.13. Netflix Organizational Change & Structure Case Study 2022

Available From: https://wp.kennisbanksocialeinnovatie.nl/wp-content/uploads/2022/09/Netflixorganizationalchange.pdf

4.14. Netflix Firm's Change Management and Organizational Structure

Available From: https://business-essay.com/netflix-firms-change-management-and-organizational-structure/

4.15. Netflix: Valuing a New Business Model Change Management Analysis & Solution

Available From: http://fernfortuniversity.com/hbr/change-management/1274-netflix-streaming.php

4.16. From DVDs to streaming, here's the incredible history of Netflix

Available From: https://interestingengineering.com/culture/the-fascinating-history-of-netflix

4.17. Netflix Culture: How it Redefined Employee Success

Available From: https://venngage.com/blog/netflix-culture/

4.18. How Netflix Reinvented HR

Available From: https://hbr.org/2014/01/how-netflix-reinvented-hr

4.19. How Netflix does Performance Management, 360 Feedback, & Rewards

Available From: https://www.performyard.com/articles/how-netflix-does-performance-management

4.20. What is Behind the Magic of Netflix Company Culture? - Liberty Mind

Available From: https://libertymind.co.uk/what-is-behind-the-magic-of-netflix-company-culture/

4.21. Building A Winning Workplace Culture - Revisiting the Netflix Culture Memo (careermp.com)

Available From: https://blog.careermp.com/building-a-winning-culture-revisiting-the-netflix-culture-memo

4.22. Business Insider: Netflix insiders describe how its 360 feedback reviews work.

Available From: https://www.businessinsider.com/netflix-insiders-describe-how-its-360-feedback-reviews-work-2020-3

4.23. Corporate Rebels: Employee Feedback at Netflix: 4 Powerful Guidelines.

Available From: https://www.corporate-rebels.com/blog/feedback-at-netflix

4.24. Netflix Feedback Culture: The 4-Steps to Success.

Available From: https://www.shortform.com/blog/netflix-feedback-culture/

4.25. How to give feedback, the Netflix way

Available From: https://www.strategypunk.com/how-to-give-feedback-the-netflix-way/

4.26. Learning from Netflix: How to Build a Culture of Freedom and Responsibility.

Available From: https://knowledge.wharton.upenn.edu/podcast/knowledge-at-wharton-podcast/how-netflix-built-its-company-culture/

4.27. Peter Kang: Netflix Culture Deck: 7 Slides to Remember.

Available From: https://www.peterkang.com/netflix-culture-deck-7-slides-to-remember/

4.28. Netflix: Inclusion Takes Root at Netflix: Our First Report.

Available From: https://about.netflix.com/en/news/netflix-inclusion-report-2021

4.29. Netflix: Our Progress on Inclusion: 2021 Update.

Available From: https://about.netflix.com/en/news/our-progress-on-inclusion-2021-update

4.30. Deadline: Netflix's First Inclusion Report Offers Look At Workforce Diversity.

Available From: https://deadline.com/2021/01/netflix-report-diversity-inclusion-represetation-workforce-1234672065/

4.31. Netflix Jobs

Available From: https://jobs.netflix.com/culture

4.32. Data Science at Netflix: How Advanced Data & Analytics Helps Netflix Generate Billions

Available From: https://www.aidataanalytics.network/data-science-ai/articles/data-science-at-netflix-how-advanced-data-analytics-helped-netflix-generate-billions

4.33. Netflix Change Management Case Study | Important Lessons

Available From: https://changemanagementinsight.com/netflix-change-management-case-study/

4.34. 5 Ways Netflix Uses Data to Win the World of Streaming Entertainment (lineate.com)

Available From: https://www.lineate.com/technology-insights/5-ways-netflix-uses-data-to-win

4.35. How Netflix Uses Data. Case Study | by Morgan Dougherty | Medium

Available From: https://medium.com/@tug32381/how-netflix-uses-data-5634c59a9cdc

4.36. 8 'Golden' HR Strategy Lessons From Netflix (consultport.com)

Available From: https://consultport.com/for-companies/8-golden-hr-strategy-lessons-from-netflix/

4.37. Strategic HR and CEO at Netflix

Available From: https://papersowl.com/examples/strategic-hr-and-ceo-at-netflix/

4.38. Netflix HRD: 'How I found the Holy Grail of HR' | HRD America

Available From: https://www.hcamag.com/us/specialization/hr-technology/netflix-hrd-how-i-found-the-holy-grail-of-hr/312395

4.39. The Unfolding of Netflix's Exceptional Company Culture – Values Institute

Available From: https://values.institute/the-unfolding-of-netflixs-exceptional-company-culture/

4.40. Netflix: number of subscribers worldwide 2023 | Statista

Available From: https://www.statista.com/statistics/250934/quarterly-number-of-netflix-streaming-subscribers-worldwide/

Chapter 5

5.1. The Spotify Model for Scaling Agile | Atlassian

Available From: https://www.atlassian.com/agile/agile-at-scale/spotify

5.2. Squad Health Check model - visualizing what to improve - Spotify Engineering : Spotify Engineering (atspotify.com)

Available From: https://engineering.atspotify.com/2014/09/squad-health-check-model/

5.3. Getting More from Your Team Health Checks - Spotify Engineering: Spotify Engineering (atspotify.com)

Available From: https://engineering.atspotify.com/2014/09/squad-health-check-model/

5.4. 10 Reasons for Agility Success at Spotify | by Kate Dames | Medium

Available From: https://funficient.medium.com/10-reasons-for-agility-success-at-spotify-453516a35201

5.5. The Spotify Agile Model Explained: Principles & Takeaways

Available From: https://www.appvizer.com/magazine/operations/project-management/spotify-agile-model

5.6. Spotify Agile Model: What it is and How it Works

Available From: https://www.tcgen.com/agile/spotify-agile-model/

5.7. Spotify Agile - Agile frameworks

Available From: https://agile-frameworks.com/_spotify/spotify.html

5.8. What is the Spotify Model?

Available From: https://kanbanize.com/blog/spotify-model/

5.9. Spotify and Agile - A Case Study on Agile Environments

Available From: https://www.professionaldevelopment.ie/spotify-and-agile-a-case-study-on-agile-environments

5.10. Spotify Agile Methodology. The Spotify model is a software

Available From: https://justarobot.medium.com/spotify-agile-methodology-e974f0204b97

5.11. What is the Agile Spotify Model? - Product HQ

Available From: https://producthq.org/agile/agile-spotify-model/

5.12. Spotify Agile Model Explained - Objective Based

Available From: https://objectivebased.blog/spotify-agile-model-explained/

5.13. Leadership at Spotify | Agile Alliance

Available From: https://www.agilealliance.org/resources/sessions/leadership-at-spotify/

5.14. Key Elements of Spotify's Agile Scaling Model

Available From: https://www.altigee.com/magazine/spotify-agile-model-elements-principles-and-takeaways

Chapter 6

6.1. Toyota Production System | Vision & Philosophy | Company | Toyota Motor Corporation Official Global Website

Available From: https://global.toyota/en/company/vision-and-philosophy/production-system/

6.2. Toyota Way 2020 / Toyota Code of Conduct

Available From: https://global.toyota/en/company/vision-and-philosophy/toyotaway_code-of-conduct/?padid=ag478_from_right_side

6.3. Jidoka - Toyota Production System guide - Toyota UK Magazine

Available From: https://mag.toyota.co.uk/jidoka-toyota-production-system/

6.4. Toyota Virtual Plant Tour: Toyota Production System | Toyota Virtual Plant Tour | Company | Toyota Motor Corporation Official Global Website

Available From: https://global.toyota/en/company/plant-tours/production-system/

6.5. Relationship with the Employee

Available From: https://www.toyota-industries.com/csr/reports/items/p47-52.pdf

6.6. How Toyota Pulls Improvement from the Front Line (hbr.org)

Available From: https://hbr.org/2011/06/how-toyota-pulls-improvement-f

6.7. 13 pillars of the Toyota Production System - Toyota UK Magazine

Available From: https://mag.toyota.co.uk/13-pillars-of-the-toyota-production-system/

6.8. Toyota Production System: 14 Solid Principles - Lean Six Sigma Belgium

Available From: https://leansixsigmabelgium.com/blog/toyota-six-sigma-14-solid-principles/

6.9. The Toyota Way

Available From: https://www.toyota-europe.com/about-us/toyota-vision-and-philosophy/the-toyota-way

6.10. (Still) learning from Toyota - McKinsey

Available From: https://www.mckinsey.com/industries/automotive-and-assembly/our-insights/still-learning-from-toyota

6.11. Liker, Jeffrey K. (2004). The Toyota Way: 14 Management Principles from the World's Greatest Manufacturer. McGraw-Hill.

https://www.goodreads.com/book/show/161789.The_Toyota_Way

6.12. What Really Makes Toyota's Production System Resilient

Available From: https://hbr.org/2022/11/what-really-makes-toyotas-production-system-resilient

6.13. 14 Principles of Lean Toyota Production System (TPS)

Available From: https://flevy.com/blog/14-principles-of-lean-toyota-production-system-tps/

6.14. LEAN = TPS {KAIZEN + RESPECT}

Available From: https://www.lean.org/the-lean-post/articles/lean-tps-kaizen-respect/

6.15. 7 Wastes of lean – How to eliminate all non-value-added activities?

Available From: https://www.spica.com/blog/7-wastes-of-lean

6.16. Reducing Waste and Inefficiency in Health Care Through Lean Process Redesign: Literature Review

Available From: https://www.ahrq.gov/research/findings/final-reports/leanprocess/leanprocess.html

6.17. The Toyota Culture of Continuous Improvement

Available From: https://www.reliableplant.com/Read/10817/toyota-continuous-improvement

6.18. Value Chain Collaboration

Available From: https://global.toyota/en/sustainability/esg/partners/

6.19. Remarkable Supplier Relationships are Built on Story, Strategy and Systems

Available From: https://www.business2community.com/product-management/remarkable-supplier-relationships-are-built-on-story-strategy-and-systems-02105258

6.20. TMC Announces Personnel Changes in Senior Management

Available From: https://global.toyota/en/newsroom/corporate/33557852.html

6.21. TMC Announces Changes to Executive Structure, Senior Management Responsibilities, and Personnel

Available From: https://global.toyota/en/newsroom/corporate/32997359.html

6.22. Analyzing Toyota's Recipe for Success - The Toyota Way - MBA Knowledge Base

Available From: https://www.mbaknol.com/operations-management/analyzing-toyotas-recipe-for-success-the-toyota-way/

6.23. The Toyota Production System

Available From: https://matt-rickard.com/toyota-software-production-system

6.24. The Toyota Production System (TPS) | Kanban Zone

Available From: https://kanbanzone.com/resources/lean/toyota-production-system/

6.25. Toyota Production System | Toyota Europe (toyota-europe.com)

Available From: https://www.toyota-europe.com/about-us/toyota-vision-and-philosophy/toyota-production-system

6.26. SC2020: Toyota Production System Supply Chain - MIT CTL

Available From: https://ctl.mit.edu/sites/default/files/Mac_TPS_thesis.pdf

6.27. Understanding the Toyota Production System - Creative Safety Supply

Available From: https://www.creativesafetysupply.com/articles/understanding-the-toyota-production-system/

6.28. What Really Makes Toyota's Production System Resilient - Harvard Business Review

Available From: https://hbr.org/2022/11/what-really-makes-toyotas-production-system-resilient

6.29. TOYOTA PRODUCTION SYSTEM BASIC HANDBOOK - Art of Lean

Available From: http://artoflean.com/wp-content/uploads/2019/01/Basic_TPS_Handbook.pdf

6.30. History of the Toyota Production System – Lean Challenge

Available From: https://www.iecieeechallenge.org/history-of-the-toyota-production-system/

Chapter 7

7.1. The new organizational knowledge management | Deloitte Insights

Available From: https://www2.deloitte.com/us/en/insights/focus/technology-and-the-future-of-work/organizational-knowledge-management.html

7.2. Workplace Relevance Report 2023 | Coveo

Available From: https://www.coveo.com/en/resources/reports/relevance-report-workplace?&utm_source=press-release&utm_medium=organic&utm_campaign=relevance-report-2022-workplace

7.3. Critical Knowledge| NASA

Available From: https://appel.nasa.gov/critical-knowledge/

7.4. Knowledge Capture and Transfer | NASA

Available From: https://appel.nasa.gov/critical-knowledge/knowledge-capture-and-transfer/

7.5. NASA Knowledge Community | NASA

Available From: https://appel.nasa.gov/critical-knowledge/nasa-knowledge-community/

7.6. Knowledge Inventory| NASA

Available From: https://appel.nasa.gov/knowledge/

7.7. Lessons Learned| NASA

Available From: https://appel.nasa.gov/lessons-learned/

7.8. Masters with Masters| NASA

Available From: https://appel.nasa.gov/masters-with-masters/

7.9. Knowledge Transfer| NASA

Available From: https://appel.nasa.gov/wp-content/uploads/2015/11/Knowledge-Transfer.pdfv

7.10. Shared Voyage| NASA

Available From: https://ntrs.nasa.gov/api/citations/20050041734/downloads/20050041734.pdf

7.11. Developing a Knowledge Management (KM) Plan| NASA

Available From: https://appel.nasa.gov/wp-content/uploads/2018/04/Developing-a-KM-Plan_V3.pdf

7.12. NASA Knowledge Capture and Transfer: A Guide for the Departee| NASA

Available From: https://appel.nasa.gov/wp-content/uploads/2022/03/kct-departee-guide.pdf

7.13. NASA Knowledge Capture and Transfer: A Guide for the Incoming Member| NASA

Available From: https://appel.nasa.gov/wp-content/uploads/2022/03/kct-incoming-member-guide.pdf

7.14. NASA Knowledge Capture and Transfer: A Guide for Supervisors | NASA

Available From: https://appel.nasa.gov/wp-content/uploads/2022/03/kct-supervisors-guide.pdf

7.15. Virtual Backgrounds | NASA

Available From: https://appel.nasa.gov/courses/virtual-backgrounds/

7.16. Taxonomy and Metadata | NASA

Available From: https://appel.nasa.gov/wp-content/uploads/2015/11/Taxonomy-and-Metadata2.pdf

7.17. Quick Webinars | NASA

Available From: https://appel.nasa.gov/watch-listen-learn/quick-webinars/

7.18. Search and Findability | NASA

Available From: https://appel.nasa.gov/wp-content/uploads/2015/11/Search-and-Findability.pdf

7.19. Knowledge Management Process | NASA

Available From: https://appel.nasa.gov/wpcontent/uploads/2015/11/Storytelling.pdf

7.20. Reflective Practice | NASA

Available From: https://appel.nasa.gov/wp-content/uploads/2015/11/Reflective-Practice.pdf

7.21. Social Networks | NASA

Available From: https://appel.nasa.gov/wp-content/uploads/2015/11/Social-Networks.pdf

7.22. Knowledge Management Process | NASA

Available From: https://appel.nasa.gov/wpcontent/uploads/2015/11/Knowledge-Management-Process.pdf

7.23. Knowledge Audit | NASA

Available From: https://appel.nasa.gov/wpcontent/uploads/2015/11/Knowledge-Audit.pdf

7.24. Case Studies | NASA

Available From: https://appel.nasa.gov/wp-content/uploads/2015/11/Case-Studies_V2.pdf

7.25. Gamification | NASA

Available From: https://appel.nasa.gov/wpcontent/uploads/2015/11/Gamification.pdf

7.26. Diversity of Thought | NASA

Available From: https://appel.nasa.gov/wp-content/uploads/2015/11/Diversity-of-Thought.pdf

7.27. Developing a Knowledge Management (KM) Plan

Available From: https://appel.nasa.gov/wpcontent/uploads/2018/04/Developing-a-KM-Plan_V3.pdf

7.28. Collaboration | NASA

Available From: https://appel.nasa.gov/wpcontent/uploads/2015/11/Collaboration_V2.pdf

7.29. Pause and Learn | NASA

Available From: https://appel.nasa.gov/wp-content/uploads/2015/11/After-Action-Review_V3.pdf

7.30. Knowledge Sharing Tools | NASA

Available From: https://appel.nasa.gov/knowledge/results/?_knowledge_category=knowledge-sharing-tools&_knowledge_organization=hq